VIETNAM
STORIES

DREAMS TO NIGHTMARES

To Rich,

Freedom is not free.

Red Runnell

Thank you.

VIETNAM STORIES

STORIES

DREAMS TO NIGHTMARES

–*Vietnam 1967*–

TED PANNELL

TATE PUBLISHING & *Enterprises*

Published by Tate Publishing & Enterprises, LLC
127 E. Trade Center Terrace | Mustang, Oklahoma 73064 USA
1.888.361.9473 | www.tatepublishing.com

Tate Publishing is committed to excellence in the publishing industry. The company reflects the philosophy established by the founders, based on Psalm 68:11,
"The Lord gave the word and great was the company of those who published it."

Book design copyright © 2010 by Tate Publishing, LLC. All rights reserved.
Cover design by Kellie Southerland
Interior design by Stefanie Rane
Front Cover is Ted Pannell

Published in the United States of America

ISBN: 978-1-61663-820-7
1. History, Military, Vietnam War
2. Biography & Autobiography, Military
11.01.11

DEDICATION

To my wife, Sylvia, who saved my life.

Your undying love and devotion made me a better man. I appreciate your support, diligence, and commitment to this book. You have given me a wonderful, adventurous life, and even today I never know what to expect from you. Your patience, sense of humor, and common-sense approach to life has brought me the greatest pleasure and blessing one could ever hope for. For having God joined us together, I'll be forever thankful. You have turned my "nightmares into dreams."

ACKNOWLEDGMENTS

I'd like to thank my Palm Desert writer's group, who helped make this project possible. The work of serious minds and some really talented writers: Audrey Moe, Gordon Davis, Gordon Gumpertz, Carol Johansen, John Parkington, Elize Van Zandt, and Carol Mann.

To my wife, Sylvia, and daughters, Cindy, Lindy, Lena and my sister, Linda, who have always been there for me and made my life a happy place. And to Sylvia, whose story editing and patience with me were invaluable in composing my work.

To daughter Jeana, who is far away, but near to my heart.

To Marshall Jackman, a man of God, son-in-law, and best friend, who has touched my life in many ways.

To John Bagdon, a true and wise friend, who lent his time and skill helping with the photos.

To all the men and women who proudly serve our country today, I thank you.

And finally to the Vietnam veterans who bravely sacrificed their lives. And to those who returned home with emotional and physical scares and were invisible walking through the airport. I proudly salute each and every one of you … welcome home.

TABLE OF CONTENTS

INTRODUCTION

While in army boot camp, the average age of the trainee was eighteen. They were excited and delusional, several exclaimed, "Yeah, we'll go over there and kick some VC butt." They were trained and ready. But all that changed when they got off the plane, the heat and humidity hit them in the face, and they were given weapons and sixty pounds of equipment to carry around. And when the shooting began, they froze, scared out of their minds. War didn't seem so honorable and glorious.

I came across Private Owens laying on his back, holding his severed hand across his chest, his rifle beside him in pieces. The weapon had been smashed by a bullet, ripping off his hand. Doc Ryan had already bandaged the stump, and shot him full of morphine. Owens's eyes were glossy, his face pocked with shrapnel from his shattered M-16.

He held up the dirty, detached hand. "Hey Sarge, look what I got." The morphine was working.

There were 58,148 killed and 304,000 wounded in this most unpopular war.

Some of these stories can be incredible, but they are based on real events. Anyone who has been in combat will testify that unbelievable, even spiritual things happen. It's what makes a soldier who he is…a little crazy but alive. Why does an angel seem to be watching over some and not others? Wonderful miracles happen one instant, then the horrifying work of the devil the next. It's a mystery only God knows.

If the young men survived they would come home with that unmistakable look in their eyes that said they had shook hands with the devil himself. To those who are still struggling from PTSD, don't dwell on what you can not change. I hope these stories give you inspiration and encouragement to seek happiness. Don't let your hopes and aspirations go from Dreams to Nightmares. Welcome home.

"With God, all things are possible."
— MARK 10:27 —

PROLOGUE:
DREAMS OF WAR

My wars began as a seven-year-old boy living on a dairy ranch in central California. I had two toy guns, one a silver Western cap pistol, a Christmas gift, and the other a hand-carved wooden rifle that my dad had made. I cherished both, polishing and waxing them as though they were real.

I rode a gentle old mare named Star because of the resemblance of one on her forehead. I would take her out to the pastures where our cows grazed and help my dad bring them in for the evening milking. But I wasn't just a boy on a horse; I was a cowboy herding cattle across the Texas plains, an Indian riding bareback, or a cavalryman in search of renegades. It was a great adventure.

Ted Pannell with first rifle, age 6

Whenever my dad drove to town for supplies at the grain and feed warehouse, I joined him then went next door to the army surplus store. It smelled musty of old things that had survived the war. There were large photographs on the wall of soldiers in combat that seized my imagination. I rummaged through the rows and stacks of combat gear. I hounded my dad to buy me a piece of used equipment. For my birthday, the grandest gift of all, the liner of a steel helmet. Eventually my collection included a webbed belt, a backpack, an ammo pouch, and first aid pack.

The ranch became my battleground. I crawled through the jungles of the South Pacific, took *A Walk in the Sun* in Italy, and landed on the black *Sands of Iwo Jima*. My imagination exploded. I'd make an airport in the dirt at the bottom of a tree, complete with gun bunkers, little airplanes made of sticks, and buildings out of leaves. Then I'd put rocks in a bucket, climb the tree, and sit down in the cockpit of a fighter plane. I'd make a humming engine noise, looking over the sides for the enemy below like I'd seen in the movies. Then spotting the enemy, I'd drop my bombs of rocks on them.

I joined the Cub Scouts and later became a Boy Scout, where I was made a pack leader. Summer camp was wonderful with two weeks in the mountains. We were always in our tan uniforms, cleaning our quarters, KP, first aid, and survival training, just like the army. My real love was the long march into the mountains. With my hunting knife, hatchet, and full backpack, I was a soldier searching the tree line for the enemy, and my job was to kill them and protect my men.

In 1950, photos of the Korean War began appearing in *Life* magazine. There were army infantry divisions charging across frozen fields, a tank racing through a small creek, and a solitary machine gunner sat on a hill blasting away at North Korean troops. It looked glorious, heroic. One photo stunned me to the core. It was a group of dead American soldiers lying in a ditch, hands tied behind them with wire. They had been executed by the North Koreans. Their hands were dirty, the fingers swollen twice the normal size. For the first time in my life, I felt hatred toward a people I didn't even know. How could they do such a thing as this to those good American sol-

diers? They weren't playing fair … from my youthful thinking. Years passed and I grew out of playing
army, but John Wayne was still my hero, and I loved
war movies of the 1950s. I always felt that someday I
would go to war.

At Modesto High School, football became my
great passion. To me that was a war, and the weekly
games were the battles. There was the hard physical
training, and our playbook held the plans of war. Practice was executing strategies and hand-to-hand combat to overcome the enemy. We wore uniforms and
helmets. I excelled and played first team for four years.

After graduation in 1959, a couple of my buddies joined the army, but I had no interest since there
wasn't a war. Just being a soldier wasn't for me; something had to be at stake. Like a football game, there
had to be conflict and an outcome. My goal was to
attend college, play football, and maybe the pros. But
things don't always turn out the way you plan. I went
to Los Angeles, but instead of going to school, I got
married and we had a child. My life became diapers,
baby bottles, and working two jobs. In 1964 we sepa-
rated, and I returned to Modesto and lived with my
widowed grandmother. She was young spirited and
quite active. She loved working in her yard and was
an expert seamstress, not to mention a superb cook
and baker.

When I talked of getting a job, she'd say, "You can
work later; there are plenty of things to do around
here," which was fine with me. We decided to paint
the kitchen, which for some odd reason, seemed to

take a long time. But something was missing, and it troubled me the way my life was going. I had no ambition and no positive outlook for the future, a dead ship in a calmed sea.

Between paintings, we'd stop for lunch and end up watching soaps, sitcoms, and then the Vietnam conflict, as it was called, on the evening news. I kept busy reading, taking long walks, lifting weights, and running errands. But all the while Vietnam was on my mind. I could hardly wait for the evening broadcasts to see film of the fighting, listening to the politicians trying to justify our need to be there.

Something familiar had taken hold of me; something from the past, something from my childhood. It was that photo of the American soldiers shot to death with their hands tied behind their back, a sore that had been festering for years.

Something else in the news bothered me. Young people were protesting against the war. Draftees were fleeing to Canada and burning their draft cards faster than draft notices could be sent out. Were they cowards? Were they not patriotic enough to stand with our country to fight communism? Sometimes you have to fight a bully in his yard before he comes to yours. Being married with a child, my classification was 4-F and I wouldn't be drafted. I was jobless and struggling to pay child support. Yet there was this longing to go, to see for myself what it was all about over there. But serving three or fours years in the military didn't sit well with me. I just wanted to go to Vietnam without serving a lot of extra military time. So I went to the draft board to see what my options were. The sergeant said the draft was only two years of service, and a high percentage of draftees went to Vietnam. And yes, I could volunteer for the draft. Child support could be taken out of my army pay. Perfect! He couldn't push the papers in front of me fast enough, and all he wanted to know was when I could leave.

My mother and grandmother were sad and then angry with me. "Why in the world would you do a stupid thing like that?" There was no answer, other than it was my destiny—but they wouldn't understand that. Within a month, I reported to the draft board at the post office and was put on a bus to Fort Ord, California for boot camp. I had my war.

'OLE MAN IN 'NAM

During basic training at Fort Ord, I was appointed squad leader. Probably because I was twenty-six, the oldest man in our platoon. The other trainees were an average age of eighteen, many just out of high school. When the young man who had been appointed platoon guide didn't show leadership qualities, I was promoted to his position.

From the beginning they called me Pops, the 'ole man, and anything else they could link with something older than rope. But the joke was on them; I was the one giving the orders, KP, guard duty, and extra pushups to emphasize a point.

During one point of training, our company had to prepare for a general inspection. Individual lockers, beds, uniforms, and weapons were to be in perfect order, and all eleven of the general orders were to be memorized. On the parade ground, my company was lined up by platoons, going through a mock inspection. I had never forgotten the movie *The D.I.,* where Jack Webb played a drill instructor. He would get in his trainee's face, shouting and shooting questions at them faster than they could answer. Of course it was to bring out the best of their spirit and character.

The thought came to me to do the same thing to get my platoon ready. I went down the lines, firing questions at them, checking their uniforms, boots, weapons, and everything required for the real inspection.

"Soldier, what is your first general order?"

"Platoon Leader, my first general order is, 'Take charge of this post and all government property in view.'"

"Soldier, why is there a loose string on your uniform? Are you trying to hang yourself?" If a shirt wasn't just right, I'd jerk it out of their pants, pull on a loose button, or throw a crooked cap to the ground. I was loud and stone faced, just like Jack Webb; that is until I turned to move down the next row. Standing nearby were a lieutenant and a captain watching my little performance. I was embarrassed and could feel a red heat flow up my neck to my face.

Quickly I toned it down and went back to a normal, quieter voice until the officers lost interest and went away. I never did that again. Later, the guys told me they were scared to death because the act had drawn the attention of company officers to us. Regardless, it gained me a lot of respect, and our platoon did receive very high inspection marks. Our drill instructor, Sergeant Wakii, was quite proud of us.

Wakii was a Korean War veteran from Hawaii. During our combat training, he told war stories. One in particular left us with our mouths hanging open.

"My platoon, about the size of this one," he pointed to us, "had been holding this hill top position when we were overrun by the North Korean army. In the end, it was hand to hand fighting. When I realized I was one of the last ones remaining and that we were wiped out, I pulled a dead buddy over me and smeared some of his blood on me. After the commies shot and bayoneted the wounded, they left me for dead."

No one said a word during the story, but I saw some of the boys giving each other a look of shock and awe.

"After they had left, I got out from under the body and looked for the radio, but they had taken it, so there was no way of reporting what had happened. The gooks were still in the area, so I couldn't leave there yet. I gathered weapons, ammo and moved into one of our dugout caves. I knew it was just a matter of time before someone would come checking on us if there was no reports. It was almost three weeks before anyone showed up. All the companies in the area had been overrun too. When I was finally rescued, I weight just ninety-eight pounds. I had only a few rations and very little water." He concluded by saying, "So, it was my training and the will to live that I survived. That's why it's imperative that you learn and work hard here and now, if you're going to make a good soldier, and a survivor."

He showed us his Silver and Bronze Stars, which made quite an impression on us. Needless to say, Sergeant Wakii put us into a real fighting spirit. After he left I could hear the boys vowing to take the training much more serious. Our drill instructor had just brought the real face of war to us and it wasn't a pretty sight.

By the time basic training was over, we were ready to make John Wayne proud, to avenge our Sergeant Wakii's horrible ordeal, and go kill some Viet Cong. Little did we know that war wasn't like the movies or the distant glory of medals and story telling.

After basic, several others and I from our platoon were sent to Fort Lee, Virginia for AIT, Advanced Individual Training, to be schooled as armorers or small arms specialist. I had hoped for advance infantry, but was glad to still be with some of the guys from our platoon. Classroom training was boring: breaking down weapons, repairing and cleaning them, cramming the books to learn each weapon's specs and testing. But when school was finished, we could break down any small weapon and put it back together blindfolded, which was our final test. I was glad when it was finally over.

The day after finishing AIT, two others and I received orders for Vietnam. I was surprised there hadn't been more. One poor kid was crazy with fear.

The other was being sent to language school for Vietnamese, and then he would be going to Vietnam.

I received a thirty-day leave to go home to see my family. Mom was heartbroken when it came time to leave. The gleam of going to war had lost its luster. But what was done was done.

As the chartered 707 made its final approach into Bien Hoa airbase in Vietnam, the aircraft suddenly pulled sharply upward, aborting the landing.

Jerry Pedersen, who sat in the window seat yelled, "Look, the field is being attacked."

I leaned over him and saw plumes of black smoke rising from the ground. Everyone jumped to the windows, looking into the depths of hell. I could hear guys doing a running commentary on the action below. "Wow, did you see that?"

"Damm, look at the gas tank blow."

I could see tiny figures running about then suddenly disappear in a fireball. Trucks and jeeps raced around trying to avoid incoming rockets. After a few moments the pilot announced for everyone to take their seats. Muffled sounds of the explosions faded as we climbed and turned away.

The hands of the young boy sitting next to me were shaking. "Man, what have I gotten myself into?"

I was beginning to think the same thing. I felt sick to my stomach thinking of the men I saw getting blown up, suddenly wondering how I might be killed. You would think an airbase this large would be reasonably safe, but now it hit home, no place was going to be safe in this country.

We circled for thirty minutes before landing through heavy smoke. The tarmac was covered with wreckage and smoldering carters, buildings and aircrafts were on fire, people were running and shouting with arms waving. Then I heard John Wayne's familiar voice in my head, "Welcome to Vietnam, Pilgrim." The realism of being in a war finally hit me and the thought was frightening yet exciting as I hung in a dreamlike state. One second I wanted to stay on the plane, the next I wanted to charge out there and do something. I couldn't take my eyes from the window and the mayhem going on outside. My confusion was interrupted when an army officer in the plane jumped up and yelled, "Follow me. Don't stop for anything." And follow we did, on rubber legs. A blast of hot air hit me in the face as I exited the plane. I coughed on the strong fumes of aviation fuel, oil, and other burning materials that rolled across the airfield.

In single file, we picked our way through the rubble until we came upon a smoldering shell crater. I threw my hand to my mouth to keep from throwing up when I saw two mangled, charred bodies of American soldiers. Somewhere in our group I heard gasps, and someone heaved his guts out. My legs wouldn't move fast enough to get past those poor young men.

We moved into the mess hall, a large wood and metal building. Long tables with chairs were lined up in four rows. Most of the men were silent, some quietly talked nervously. Jerry Pedersen, who had sat next to me on the plane, pulled up a chair and sat down. His hands were shaking. He was tanned with sun-bleached hair and talked about surfing. At nineteen he had planned on marrying his girlfriend when he returned home to Santa Cruz. She'd made him a bracelet of leather and beads with her name on it that he was proud to wear.

He told me of wanting to attend college on the GI bill for a career in law, which was why he enlisted in the military police before being drafted. It was different for me; I lived day to day and had no such plans beyond being in Vietnam for twelve months, if I made it that long.

Two officers gave us an hour of in-country indoctrination, and then we were dismissed to go retrieve our duffle bags unloaded from the plane and report to the barracks. Once there, we took side-by-side cots. By then it was late evening and time for chow.

Eventually Pedersen was assigned to an MP company in Saigon. Oddly, I too was assigned to a military police company attached to an infantry division. I had a sense of loss when we said good-bye. He had been the only person I'd befriended during our indoctrination.

Several replacements were taken by truck to the large base camp. But when I reported to the MP company headquarters, we discovered they already had two armorers. They had been expecting field duty replacements. I could either transfer to a unit needing an armorer or stay there and do on the job training as an MP. It was a no-brainer. I elected to stay, which made me glad. Though I had no idea what that meant, it beat the hell out of sitting in a small room smelling gun oil and handing out weapons.

After drawing my field gear, I reported to my squad's hooch. It was an underground bunker and large enough to accommodate ten men and their equipment, including cots and lockers. It smelled of dirt, canvas, and gun oil. The room was empty except for one shirtless, sandy-haired kid with a bloody nose. He greeted me with a nod and pointed to three empty cots, each with a small American flag on them.

"You can take any one of those. I gotta go." He put a rag to his nose and walked away. Not knowing what to do but wait for the squad leader, I put my equipment on one of the cots and sat down. The hooch had a wooden floor, some chairs, and a couple of tables, one with chips and playing cards, hands still in place for five players. A low hum came from two rotating fans standing at each end of the room, but it was still hot and humid.

I thought about what had just happened and concluded that I wouldn't be safe anywhere or anytime. That was terrifying. The flag on the end of the cot represented someone's dead loved one. My hands started to shake, my stomach quivered, and I felt weak.

An hour passed before men of the squad drifted in. Some wore fatigues, boots, and helmets; some were shirtless. A few acknowledged me with nods or just eye contact; others passed, faces dirty, eyes vacant. The squad leader, Sergeant Mays, who looked to be in his thirties, was the last to arrive. I tried to put on a fearless face but, I guess I didn't succeed. He introduced himself and said. "Welcome to first squad." He smiled. "You look a little green. You okay? Heard you had quite a reception, huh? Get used to it. We'll get together in a little bit. Meanwhile, put your gear away." He walked off without waiting for a reply. *Nice to meet you too.*

I was also promoted to private first class and felt honored until I found out that all privates become PFCs upon arriving in a warzone. I guess they didn't want any privates getting killed.

What we had seen coming in not only made me sick and scared, it made me angry. That anger would later become controlled rage and fear that I would accept and understand as my salvation. A force that kept me focused on what had to be done to get through the insanity.

Two days later, I was on the base camp's perimeter at a sandbag lookout post about to be introduced to a thousand screaming Viet Cong.

PEEK-A-BOO FIREFIGHT

My squad leader, Sergeant Mays, instructed me about military police duties, of convoy escorts, base camp security, and twenty-four-hour perimeter guard duty. He talked of the Vietnamese people, and our enemy, the Viet Cong, also called Charlie, and their nasty habit of wanting to kill us.

Two days later, Mays assigned me with him for night guard duty on the base camp perimeter. That evening, we geared up in our hooch. Butterflies in my stomach reminded me of suiting up before high school football games. But this time, fighting in the trenches had a whole different meaning. I had been issued an M-16 with plenty of ammo and a .45 pistol. Most of the men were silent as they checked and double-checked their weapons, ammo, grenades, extra clips, bandages, insect repellant, and rations for a long night. A low murmur and metallic clicking sounds of equipment and web gear could be heard. It was solemn, almost eerie. I was nervous and already sweating. I thought about the two bodies in the shell crater from the airbase attack. *Will I be able to do the job tonight or end up like them?* Another part of my brain was excited and eager to be tested.

We set up our position along a five-foot high wall built of timber and sandbags that looked over a 200-yard open field called the kill zone, cleared by our engineer's bulldozers. The zone was laced with barbed wire, trip flares, and claymore mines.

Mays laid out some ammo clips for his M-16 and rounds for an M-79 grenade launcher. With trembling hands I did the same, knowing I may be killing another human being soon. Two-man positions were evenly spaced twenty yards apart around the perimeter, but it was too dark to see anyone. It felt like we were out there alone.

"M-79 huh?" I said, nodding at the weapon.

"You know this thing?"

"Yeah, my MOS is armorer."

"Good, it may come in handy sometime. We'll be here a while, but don't get comfortable. Intelligence says Charlie is moving this way. So stay alert."

We talked quietly, getting to know each other while constantly scanning the field.

Sergeant Mays was thirty-three, a career soldier, and married with two kids. He joined the army at nineteen during the Korean War and fought at the battle of Pork Chop Hill with the 45th Infantry Division. I wanted to ask if he knew Sergeant Wakii, but I recanted the thought as being pretty dumb.

I told him my story of wanting to be a soldier as a kid, the John Wayne war movies and wanting to come to 'Nam. We both laughed at that. Soon we grew weary of the chitchat and fell silent. Spots began dancing in my eyes from looking into the darkness; I even thought I saw things moving. I'd jump and ready my weapon; Mays calmly placed his hand on it.

We heard someone coming down the line on our side. Mays quickly turned.

When the person got close enough to see, Mays said, "It's the company commander, Captain Ross. He's a nice guy and knows his stuff; this is his second tour."

"You boys doing okay here?" Ross said with the voice of an older man.

"Fine, sir. So far, so good," Mays said.

"Good, stay alert. We could get something tonight." The captain moved on without another word.

"By the way," Mays said, "Don't ever salute an officer in a combat zone. Charlie is just looking for that. Good way to lose our officers."

I liked Mays; he was a good soldier, smart, and I was glad to be there with him.

Later, a low, thick fog rolled across the field; the air became cool, moist, and smelled swampy.

"This is not good," Mays said quietly. "Charlie loves this shit. Stay alert."

I felt a huge furry cat turn around in my stomach. Despite the damp air, sweat formed on my hands and forehead, and my shirt stuck to my back.

About two a.m., I was trying to doze while Mays stood his turn at watch. Suddenly a rocket screamed overhead, landing with a deafting explosion somewhere in the compound.

"Up, up," yelled Mays. "It's happening."

I sprung up, my head and shoulder well above the wall. This time Mays grabbed my shoulder and pushed down hard. I got the message.

Green tracers streamed at us out of the haze looking like a laser show. AK-47s, grenades, and mortar rounds popped all around us or fell short.

Immediately, the sky lit up with our flares, illuminating the field, but all I could see was the white fog. Then there were sounds that rattled me down to my toes: yelling, whistles, and bugles. Out of the mist came hundreds of screaming, ghostlike figures. Adding to the confusion, the flares on parachutes rocked back and forth, the scene like an old, flickering black and white film; phantom shadows moving everywhere.

"Hold your fire until they get closer!" Mays shouted.

Mortar rounds from our side sailed overhead, slamming among the charging Cong. To the right and left, our M-60 and .50-caliber machine guns opened up with a roar. Endless sheets of steel, like an orange monster swallowed the little people whole and spit them out in pieces. It was an in-your-face fireworks killing show like I'd never seen before.

Small arms and automatic weapon rounds hammered into our position like a hive of super bees, ripping holes into the sandbags and logs, sending sand and splinters into our faces.

I ducked down to wipe sand from my eyes. What I'd thought was sweat, was blood from bits of wood embedded in my face. Mays stayed crouched, his eyes and helmet just above the wall, watching everything.

"Get up here and get ready; they're almost close enough."

I rose to a squatting position, readied my weapon, and stared at the shrieking Cong and froze. They were throwing their bodies across the barbed wire, allowing others to use them as a bridge. The raiders were torn apart by exploding, trip-wire claymore mines and mortar rounds. Our machine gun rounds ripped off clothing and chunks of flesh from the charging boyish bodies.

Sounds were deafening causing me to become disorientated, terrified beyond words at the sight, my heart felt ready to burst.

Mays yelled, "Now! Fire!"

I squeezed the trigger, but nothing happened. I squeezed again and again, still nothing. I went down behind the wall hardly able to breath. Inspecting my weapon, I found the safety on. I'd been so scared I'd forgotten to take it off. Mays yelled something, but I couldn't hear above the noise. Suddenly, he moved away, firing frantically to our right flank. My head began to clear. With trembling hands, I released the safety, flipped on full automatic, placed the weapon on top of the wall, and fired over my head without looking.

I felt something hit my ass hard. I turned to see Captain Ross crouched there with a .45 in his hand. "What are you doing, playing peek-a-boo? Get up there and look where you're shooting, soldier, before you shoot our own guys!" he yelled, and then he moved down the wall. My legs were like jelly, but somehow I rose to the top of the wall and was shocked to see mangled bodies lying in front of me; dark blood soaked tan uniforms of the NVA, body parts torn away. The Cong were now moving to the right and left of me, like the sea crashing around a rock. Closing my eyes I fired a burst into a small group. When I looked, two were dead on the ground; two others were bloody, but still attempting to fire towards our line. This time I took aim and finished them off like you would a dying animal. This was how I now felt, like they were animals.

To my left, they overran our position. There was popping explosions of small arms fire, yelling and screaming of hand-to-hand sadistic warfare, cries of suffering, frenzied and furious fighting … bayonets, trenching shovels, and hatchets flashed in the moonlight, the sickening scent of sulfur gun powder, the awful stench of death.

The breakthrough was repelled and the shooting tapered off with random shots, and I heard "Cease fire!" from down the line. Heavy smoke from mortars and other explosives hung in the air, my eyes stung, my ears rang, and my clothes were soaking wet. I took a deep breath, but I only got thick smells of sulfur that almost made me vomit.

It was hard to comprehend what had just occurred, what I had just done. It happened so fast. I hadn't given much thought of taking a life, yet in a matter of seconds, I'd taken several. It was mind numbing. War was nothing like I'd ever imagined; it was loud, gruesome, and ugly, and I was aghast with fear.

Looking around for Sergeant Mays, he appeared out of the smoke, holding a bloody bandage to his neck.

He glanced over the wall. "Good job, they didn't get through. Are you okay?"

"Yeah, what happened to you?"

"Just a scrape, it could have been worse. Tomorrow, you'll see the chaplain."

"Why?"

"Ever kill anyone?"

"No."

'How do you feel?"

"I don't know … it's … I'm … " Bile laced my throat, and I quickly turned away and threw up.

"That's why," Mays said softly. "The chaplain's a good man. You did good tonight."

Mays smiled and pointed with his rifle to my pants. "What happened there … a little scared were you?"

I looked down and found I had pissed my pants.

SHOT IN THE DARK

After the raid on our compound, my baptism by fire and killing the VC, I went to see the chaplain as Sergeant Mays had ordered. I was full of guilt and I wondered how the chaplain would deal with my struggle and pain.

The Chaplin's quarters were a small tent walled with sandbags and some cut tree logs. It accommodated a cot, desk and a small file cabinet, like all base camp quarters, it smelled of musky dirt.

Captain Chambers was tall and thin, with kind blue eyes looking at me from a tan face. He appeared to be about thirty-five. "Well, I guess we know why you're here, pretty ugly out there last night. Tough times call for tough action, but it's never easy when it comes to dealing with death." He picked up the bible and flipped through the pages. "Matthew and even Exodus says, 'Blessed are the peacemakers, for they will be called the children of God.' Mind if I ask if you are a Christian?"

"From an early age I went to a small country church and believe in God. I've always felt He is with me. But I haven't been to church in some time."

"You are a peacemaker and a child of God. What you did last night wasn't wrong. You are a soldier doing a soldier's job. The bible does say, 'You shall not murder.' But the Hebrew word literally means 'the intentional, premeditated killing of another person with malice.' You did not murder last night, my son. You were protecting your life and that of other men. Self defense killing is not a sin. Neither is killing in a 'justified' war. There was no malice in your actions. A soldier who commits to defend their country is doing his civil duty. Even God sent his armies to kill in righteous wars, justified wars. You're justified as long as you are in God's army." He smiled. "And as long as you are in the United States Army."

"But what about this guilt and aching in my heart?"

"That will disappear in time. There are other things in war and being a soldier than just killing. Someday, you will do good, maybe to a child, or save a life. Remember, though I walk through the valley of death I fear no evil, for God and my M-16 comfort me." He smiled again. At least someone had a sense of humor about war.

Captain Chambers concluded by praying for me and I left there feeling less guilty and more justified. I was a soldier now, doing what a soldier has to do, but the aching in my heart remained. Anyway, throughout the rest of my tour, I said a lot of prayers.

A few days later, we were attached to a 9th Infantry base camp in the Mekong Delta. We would participate in a joint mission with the infantry on an overnight ambush patrol. It wasn't unusual to pull these assignments when we were needed, though none of us liked this type of duty. We preferred doing what we did best, escort and defend convoys.

We gathered to check our weapons and gear, and I couldn't help notice how calm and laid back the infantrymen were, quietly talking and laughing, applying black and green paste to their faces. Some grunts had written words on their helmets with magic markers, such as, Born to Kill, Mass Murderer, Hired Gun, Serial Killer, and Gunfighter.

At dusk, we fell in behind the infantry patrol down a path leading into the jungle. Very quickly the vegetation closed around us and grew darker the deeper we went. It was hot and humid and I was already sweating. There was the pungent smell of swamp, stagnant water from the rainfall. Mosquitoes and flies were relentless to exposed skin.

A "no talking" order had been given, and the only sounds were footsteps, an occasional bug slap to the skin, or a muffled cursing. We'd taped down our dog tags from rattling and restrained any equipment that might make noise.

We walked about half a mile, and then stopped at a small clearing. The lieutenant come up to Mays, whispered something and returned to his men.

Mays signaled us to form up. "This is it," he whispered, then pointed. "Spread out in this area. The grunts are setting up the ambush there along the trail. Once you're in position, sit down; don't move or make a sound. Charlie should come down that trail. But he could come from any direction, so stay alert; no sleeping."

I found a comfortable place against a tree. The infantry changed into bush hats, preparing for the ambush. Carefully, they set up claymore trip mines and trip flares with practiced ease, and then they faded into the foliage like green reptiles.

In what seemed like an instant, it got so dark I couldn't see my hand in front of me. I fingered the automatic switch on the M-16 to semi. This wasn't a place to be spraying a full magazine, at least not yet. The butterflies danced in my stomach, anticipating the looming danger.

Hours passed; my butt hurt. I squirmed and wiggled, mosquitoes attacked my sweating face, and ants bit my hands. I was more afraid of snakes than the VC at that moment. Somehow, I managed to stay composed. The nocturnal jungle animals and birds were carrying on a huge symphony. I jumped at every little sound. To this day, I don't like the dark.

Even with all the tension, I thought about home, my family, some girls, and buddies ... what were they doing at this moment as I sat there waiting to kill someone. I had accepted the thought and tried to compare it to a professional hunter, except my target could shoot back.

My eyes finally adjusted to the darkness and could barely make out the clearing; there was no sign of Charlie or anyone else. It was spooky and lonely. Suddenly, a noise sent a yellow streak up my spine and exploded in my brain. Something was moving to my right, not on the trail, but coming toward me. I listened intently, strained my eyes, and fingered my weapon. Who or what was it ... should I challenge? I waited. The sound continued to move closer. I shouldered my rifle. What was the code word? Oh yeah— *Cracker*—the answer was Jack.

I whispered, "Cracker." No answer. "Cracker." Nothing.

It came closer. I couldn't wait any longer and fired a short burst in that direction. There was a moan ... the sound of falling into the brush, another moan, then silence.

No one moved. They must have been scared to death too, but they kept their cool. My hands shook, sweat burned my eyes, and I wondered what I'd just done.

The rest of the night was quiet except for the sounds of monkeys, frogs, birds, and whatever else inhabited this place. I couldn't stop thinking about what I'd done, and I said a short prayer that I hadn't shot my own man.

Charlie hadn't showed, and I was so thankful. Gradually the blackness lifted, and the jungle came alive with sounds of early morning. Soon, the lieutenant appeared in the clearing, calling "Clear." Men emerged from the foliage like creatures of the earth.

Mays was at my side. "Let's take a look," he said.

We went a few yards and stopped. He snickered.

"Nice shooting, Buffalo Bill," he said, followed with a full laugh.

I looked down and there laid a water buffalo. The boys never let me forget that.

Like the water buffalo in story, called a Vietnamese tractor.

NO JOYRIDE

Convoy escort duty in Vietnam could be uneventful, dangerous, or deadly, but never boring. On one of these runs, I was riding point jeep. PFC Gilbert was our driver, and Sergeant Melcume was senior man in the passenger seat. I was a Spec 4, managing the M-60 in the back. I stood most of the time, but occasionally sat on the PRC 10 radio.

It was monsoon season, the day hot and muggy. My clothes stuck to my skin, and mud from the road splattered my helmet and goggles.

Ted waiting for the convoy.

I became uneasy as we approached the Hai Vang Pass. Ambushes had occurred here before. My heart raced at anything that moved or a flash of light from the hills. We came to a sharp turn; driver Gilbert slowed down. I stood and turned to check the convoy.

There was a deafening explosion, and simultaneously a huge blast of heat and dirt slammed against my upper back. I felt my head jerk backward, my body lifting...

Convoy getting ready.

I woke up in a temporary field hospital. The first thing I saw was the tent ceiling—the smell of canvas and alcohol. An IV needle was taped to my arm. There were wood-slat floors and wood sides. I could see the tops of sandbags over the five-foot walls. The canvas sides were rolled up and a hot breeze wafted through. About twelve beds were across the room and the same on my side.

A GI had one of his legs slung up in a cast, another man with a head bandage. Most men lay silent or made an occasional low moan. But over all it was peaceful, quiet.

Fans stood oscillating at each end of the large tent. I wondered, *What the hell? Why was I here? What happened? Was I dying?*

A female nurse came down the aisle smiling. She was about my age, twenty-six, pretty, with short, chestnut hair.

"Well you're finally awake," she said. "I'm Lieutenant Prescott."

"What happened, am I okay?"

"Yes, you'll be fine now that you're awake. You don't remember?"

"No. I just remember a loud blast."

"Well, you're a lucky man, Specialist. Your jeep hit a landmine."

I felt my legs; they were there. "So why am I here?"

She smiled. "A concussion and a bloody nose. Apparently, you were blown out of the jeep and landed on your face. The blast probably knocked you unconscious, and the road did the rest."

I let that sink in. Yes, the convoy, point jeep, the bend in the road.

"What happened to my buddies?"

"They'll be okay, but not as lucky as you. They had to be taken to Saigon for surgery, lots of shrapnel in their legs, some in the upper torso. Your lieutenant said it was a homemade mine, probably by VC gorillas. Had it been the NVA, you may not be here."

"You've been out since they brought you in yesterday. We cauterized your nose vessels to stop the bleeding. There was so much blood you looked dead." Prescott seemed amused.

"Was the convoy ambushed?"

"I guess. The lieutenant didn't say much."

"So, do I get a Purple Heart and sent home?"

"That's not up to me," she snapped. "If hearts were given for every superficial wound that came through here, there would be more paperwork than saving lives. You'll be going back to your unit tomorrow."

"But the blast...the VC." I tried to rise, but a terrific pain shot through my head. "And my head hurts."

Prescott looked unsympathetic. "I can get you something to eat," she said kind of officially.

"Yes, thank you."

She left quickly. I was just trying to make light of the situation. But she was clearly pissed, probably because I mentioned the Purple Heart and having only a bloody nose and a headache was hardly worth mentioning. I felt foolish.

I lay back and rubbed my temples feeling guilty. I thought of the poor boys that lost limbs or other life altering wounds. Then thankful I just had a headache. I could use the rest and may as well make the best of it.

I wondered about PFC Gilbert and Sergeant Melcume's wounds. They really deserved the heart and to be going home. I had to go back into that hellhole, maybe leaving with greater injuries or in a box. I needed an aspirin...

I stared at the tent ceiling and quickly forgot all about getting the medal. For some strange reason, I thought of the convicts back in the states—they were in air-conditioned rooms, getting the best of care, TVs, weight rooms, libraries, and weekly visits by their loved ones.

And what do us ground forces get for serving our country, for the fighting, the physical and mental wounds, and death? A tent hospital and a fan, sleeping in muddy holes, eat out of cans, and see your buddies die. Now I really felt bad for what I said.

Lieutenant Prescott returned with a tray of food. "I'm sorry Specialist. I didn't mean to come on so strong, but ... "

"No, please, I'm the one who should apologize. I wasn't thinking. I was trying to be funny."

"It's just that we see so many young men who've been ... its heart wrenching. They ... "

"I understand, Lieutenant. I don't envy your job here, and I admire your service a great deal. I just wasn't thinking. It was my first time being blown up." I smiled.

Prescott smiled back. "Thank you. Let's forget it." She placed the tray on a table beside the bed. "I brought you something special." She nodded to a bowl of ice cream and four pills on the tray.

"Codeine," she said and touched my hand. "And I admire what you do, Specialist. I know it's not easy for you either. Maybe we should all look for a little humor."

We talked and laughed for several minutes; then she said she had to get back to work. I enjoyed the dinner and ice cream, but I enjoyed being with Prescott more. The food was much better then eating beans and weenies from a can. I took two of the pills and drifted off into a haze, with flashes of being home, of girls, school buddies, and my family. The image of my baby daughter came with questions, of what went wrong with my marriage, of how much I longed for the right woman and family of my own.

Somewhere in the distance, a 105 Howitzer began registering for a night battle. Then a couple of Huey gun ships joined the mêlée. I was thankful to be here.

I was wakened early the next morning to the sound of a metal tray being placed beside my bed.

It was Prescott. "Don't you ever sleep?" I said.

"Not much. How are you feeling?"

"Great. Thanks for the dinner and the meds. I got some much-needed rest."

"Good. I thought you'd like that." She smiled. "A medevac is here to take you and a couple others back to your base camp. So eat up. I'll get your clothes."

The food was pretty decent behind the lines. I wished I was staying a couple more days, especially with Prescott being there. But what do you want for a bloody nose.

Prescott returned with my clothes in a bundle. They were still bloody and dirty with some new ventilated holes in them.

"Say, Lieutenant, you didn't wash my uniform," I said, smiling and holding them up.

"I'm sorry, Specialist. I was busy cooking your dinner. I'll call the valet."

"See there? There can be some humor in war." She grinned big and put out her hand. "Take care of yourself. I wouldn't want to see you back here again … nothing personal."

I took her hand. "Thanks for everything. You're the real hero here. You take care of yourself too, Lieutenant."

Prescott smiled and walked away. I felt my heart sink. For a while it was a touch of civilization, a slow waltz with sanity and the gentle touch of an angel of war. Again I hear the distant thunder of battle, a calling I sadly could not avoid.

THE PATROL AND
THE PRAYER

My squad set out on a one day sweep with an infantry platoon in the La Drang River valley, the western sector of Pleiku Province. Though the men of my squad were an average age of nineteen, they were already battle tested. I had full confidence in these young warriors. I'd been in country ten months, made E4, and was promoted to squad leader.

Packed light with C-rations for one day and plenty of water and ammo, we gathered with the cavalry platoon just inside the front gate, and then we moved out of the base camp in single file on a trail that lead into a dense forest. It was 100 degrees with the usual high humidity. The going was torture. Red earth stuck to our boots. Our uniforms soaked with sweat clung to our backs and chaffed our legs. Bugs and thick undergrowth between tightly netted trees made movement miserable. Sharp spines on bushes grabbed at our jungle fatigues or slashed any exposed skin. In some places the lead men had to swing their machetes to cut the trail.

After several hours, I was relieved when we finally reached the edge of the tree line. Beyond lay a vast open area of waist-high elephant grass. Here and there were small trees and a few abandoned massive ant hills reaching five to six feet high. A light wind rocked the grass like waves in a yellow sea.

Lieutenant Marcus ordered a break. Soldiers sat down where they stood or leaned against trees. Marcus called the squad leaders together for a briefing on crossing the dangerous-looking landscape too vast to go around.

After a few minutes, we were ordered to move out. I scanned the young faces of my squad. It was hard to imagine that some of these teenagers could be proficient killers. Even I didn't know what I was capable of doing until my own baptism by fire.

I gave the arm signal to move out and keep low, making us smaller targets. The thick, dry grass made it difficult to see where we stepped, and it was all that much harder to keep focused on what was in front of us.

To make matters worse, we were walking into the sun … a recipe for disaster. I pulled my helmet as low as possible to shield my eyes and still be able to see.

Suddenly a loud volley of small arms and automatic weapons fire erupted directly ahead. We had walked into a VC ambush. I couldn't see the Cong, only muzzle flashes. The grass snapped and crackled as rounds zipped through it. Adrenaline moved through me like a flash flood.

Flopped on the ground, I couldn't see the rest of my men. But for sure the enemy was directly in front of us. We returned fire, aiming waist high through the grass at the muzzle flashes just in case Charlie came charging at us.

The deafening fire continued for three or four minutes and then tapered off to random shots and finally stopped. Cries of pain and agony came from the platoon's position. One young voice cried out for his mother, "Mama, oh Mama." I knew from past experience he was probably dying. I called the medic, Spec 4 Ryan, to come forward.

Before I could catch my breath, the VC opened up again. Green tracer rounds zinged through the air, I smelled smoke. Either the tracers had caught the dry grass on fire or the Cong had purposely set it. The blowing wind created a roar and whipped the flames toward us.

If we stood up, we'd be cut down. If we stayed put, the flames would overcome us. No one could blame me for withdrawing my men, but I needed to get permission. I crawled around looking for Billy Ray, an eighteen-year-old radioman. The ground was hot and dusty. Dirt stuck to my sweaty face and filled my nostrils; rifle smoke hung low. It was hard to see anything until I was upon it. I found a soldier from another squad moaning, blood oozing from an ugly gut wound. Not far from him was a body almost ripped apart from a dozen bullets, the mouth and eyes open in shock.

I came across Private Owens, laying on his back, holding his severed hand across his chest, his rifle beside him in pieces. The weapon had been smashed by a bullet, ripping off his hand. Doc Ryan had already bandaged the stump and shot him full of morphine. Owens's eyes were glossy, his face pocked with shrapnel from his shattered M-16.

He held up the dirty, detached hand. "Hey, Sarge, look what I got." The morphine was working.

Those not wounded hugged the ground and returned fire. I found Ryan, his back to the incoming rounds treating another soldier, shielding the man with only his flack jacket and helmet.

"Ryan, you seen Billy Ray?"

He pointed. "Yeah, he's been hit, back over there."

"I need that radio."

"No good, Sarge. The radio got it too; it's out."

Smoke from the burning grass made it hard to breathe as the flames whipped closer and closer.

Since I couldn't radio Marcus for permission to withdraw, my decision was clear. It was about two hundred meters back to the trees. I'd rather die standing up than lying down. I said a short, simple prayer. "Father, please protect us all as we move out of this deadly battle. Amen."

The flames were now upon us; the heat stung my face. There was one saving grace; the smoke allowed us some cover. As I stood, a strange feeling came over me, like a protective bubble. My fear was gone, in spite of the arsenal of steel that filled the air like a pouring thunder storm.

The noise seemed to melt away. I could clearly hear the cries and voices of the men, and my own voice seemed louder.

Moving about, I ordered the wounded to be gathered up. "Don't leave anyone behind, and don't stop until we get to the tree line."

I grabbed one boy, PFC Jeffery Carmichael, who was still crying out for his mother. Blood poured from two ugly holes in his side and shoulder, and a piece of his cheek was gone. He screamed as I picked him up, but still he did his best to help me. American helmets begin appearing above the grass. Some men fired their weapons with one hand, dragging a buddy with the other.

I could feel heat from the flames on the back of my neck. I kept moving, shouting to the others while dragging Carmichael. It seemed forever, but we finally made it. There was good cover among the trees and two of the large ant hills that made a defense perimeter.

Gradually the squad scrambled in, falling with exhaustion, coughing, and bleeding. I took a quick count. Every man was there. A survey with Doc Ryan gave us three seriously wounded and three with minor grazes. The dead soldier was from Marcus's platoon.

The Cong broke off the fight, and the fire died out when it hit the sandy area of the ant hills. Another radioman came stumbling in and I called Marcus, giving him a situation report. He said the platoon was pulling back and that he had already called for a medevac. Some men went out and attached grenades and other explosives to surrounding trees to blow them up. It didn't take long for them to drag broken branches and clear an area for the LZ, landing zone, for the chopper.

I leaned against a tree, drained, shaken, soaked with sweat and blood from Carmichael. Sunlight filtered down through the trees like light shining through stained glass windows. It was a miracle that the whole squad hadn't been wiped out. But I knew it was the work of God. I lowered my head and gave him thanks.

The words of the Chaplin came to me; *someday you will do good, maybe to a child, or save a life.* I guess this was what he was talking about.

SNAKES IN THE MIX

"Snakes! Did someone say snakes were out there?" I said with a chill streaking up my spine. I hated snakes since seeing them attack people in the movies.

"Yeah, the lieutenant said this area is known for lots of snakes and to watch out for them on the patrol tonight," said PFC Clinton, a twenty-year-old towhead from Georgia.

"Not scared of a little 'ole snake are you, Sarge?" Jonesy, from Oklahoma, added.

We had moved into a new base camp on a mountaintop in the central highlands and were preparing to go out that evening on a night ambush patrol. The thought of sitting all night in the jungle with snakes was chilling; maybe one would crawl up my pant leg and slither inside my pants. Give me a fight with the VC anytime.

"Clinton, are you kiddin' me?"

"Oh yeah, Sarge. They're out there all right. I heard of a Green Beret that was bitten by a bamboo viper about this long." He held up two index fingers six inches apart. "He was dead within fifteen seconds. And I hear there are cobras and boas and no telling what else. But who knows, maybe they're all pets." The squad laughed. They enjoy a good tease to lighten the daily drama of life and death.

I knew of malaria, diseases, dysentery, quicksand, leeches, and poisonous plants that, if eaten, could kill you, and I even had heard of Bengal tigers, but this was the first I'd heard of the deadly vipers.

At the evening chow, most of the men ate in silence, focused on the night mission. We'd been together for nine months since being in country; we had lost two men. It didn't matter how many missions one goes on, you never get use to them; the nerves are always there. Some men even throw up their meal before going out.

These night ambushes were not the best or the worst of duty. A squad would set up claymore mines and trip flares along a known VC trail, then we sat and waited all night … no moving, talking, or noise of any kind, and definitely no smoking. Your spot is also your latrine. Sometimes Charlie comes, sometimes not. It can turn out to be a terrifying fight to the death or a long, boring night.

An orange sun slid behind the mountain as we gathered at the perimeter gate and double-checked our weapons and equipment. One man carries an M-79 grenade launcher, a two-man M-60 machine gun team; others carry hand grenades, claymores, M-16s, two water canteens, and helmets. Our rucksacks are light for this mission with bush hats, C-rations, and ponchos.

We moved out single-file. A few yards away from the camp, the lieutenant gave the hand signal for silence. We moved ghostlike down the narrow trail; the only sounds are of boots on dirt or the swish against grass. It's hot, the air thick. Most wear only the olive T-shirt covered with a flack vest, camouflage bandanas soaked in water wrapped around the head, faces painted in black and green stripes. Some wear sleeveless fatigue shirts. We look more like a motorcycle gang than the U.S. Infantry.

A quarter mile from the base camp, dusk settled as we set up the ambush site with the claymores, flares, some trip grenades for good measure. I moved about and arranged a frontal assault fire line with two men slightly to the rear and side to cut off any retreat. Then I checked to see that each man hadn't taken a position, as not to shoot one another.

After some pondering and close surveillance of my position, I finally sat down. *What if one of those devils slithers near me? Will I jump up and break silence ... shoot it, stab it ... scream like a girl and run?* This was starting to get to me. Better forget the damm snakes and focus on the mission.

Sweat ran from under my bush hat. My shirt was soaked under the flack jacket. One learns to move without really moving; more of a stretching technique. Or make a silent sneeze that feels like your brains might blow out through the ears.

The heavy jungle canopy makes the night even blacker. At first, I see spots and odd-looking images until my eyes adjust to the darkness. The stinking, moist swamp smell takes some getting use to. Night creatures sound eerie and then settle into an acceptable harmony, a blessing really. Should they stop, it's a warning that something is coming.

Hours later, sleep wants to come; I fight it off. Images of family and home float through my mind, and then I'm back in the jungle. Will a snake slither up to me or drop from the tree? I shudder; push it from my mind, a struggle to stay in the moment.

I doze off; my head snaps up, hearing a noise. A gray dawn seeps through the jungle awning. The lieutenant gives an all-clear whistle. One by one, ghostly figures silently materialize from the undergrowth. The men gather around me, faces gaunt with exhaustion and stress, looking much older than their youthful years.

"Well, that was a restful night," someone joked.

"Yeah, my ass is eaten up by those damm ants."

"My heat rash is back."

"I think something crawled up to me. I'm sure it was a huge snake. It made a hissing sound."

"Oh shit … look out, Sarge!"

Something is flying at me, twisting and wiggling through the air, its head turning. Someone yells, "Snake!" I scream, stumble backwards and fall. Then I hear the laughter. *What the hell?* I get up and cautiously walk back to the squad. Every man is bent over laughing and pointing to the ground. I move closer. To my surprise, and then chagrin, curled on the ground is a web belt with a stuffed sock over the end, shaped very much like a snake's head.

I smile and accept the joke with a good nature. It's good that these boy warriors can keep a sense of humor in such a grim place. That their innocence isn't completely lost, and they accept that life must go on even when death is so near. By the way, during my tour, I didn't once see a snake … thank God.

A FUN PLACE

The sunset made a mango-colored sky as we arrived at the concertina wire surrounding the kill zone to the perimeter of our company's base camp. I was bringing in the walking wounded of my eight-man squad from a three-day search and destroy mission to locate the Viet Cong.

We were flown ten miles into Easter Valley near the Demilitarized Zone, but the monsoon rains hit before we could be picked up. Thank God we didn't have KIAs to carry out.

During the operation, we checked out a village and found it to be a VC supply base. We blitzed through the village, ripping out the hut walls, dumping large baskets of fruit and vegetables, digging and probing the ground. It didn't take long to discover hiding places for large amounts of weapons, ammo, and rice.

The weapons were dumped into a nearby hole used for garbage and blown up. The village was torched along with large bundles of rice, the price paid for aiding and abetting the enemy. We moved out from the village under angry eyes of the villagers as rain clouds covered a burning sun. I radioed operations to have the villagers relocated.

A mile from the village, a light rain began. The cong appeared from nowhere and opened up on us. Caught in the open, we took causalities fast and found ourselves in the fight of our lives. We ran in every direction, diving for cover of a tree or concealing ourselves in the thick brush. Red and green tracers lasered the darkened, wet jungle.

I dove behind a palm tree, readied my M-16, and returned fire. VC rounds hit the tree and ripped up the ground around me, sending dirt, rocks, and splinters into my face. Blood blurred my vision, but I could still make out the muzzle flashes coming from the heavy undergrowth; my first clip was emptied in seconds.

Both men of our M-60 machine gun team, Taylor and Snyder, had been hit by a grenade. They were from California, only eighteen and nineteen years old, and they had bonded right away. Now Taylor had numerous fragments embedded in his face and upper body. He could only see out of one eye. Snyder had shrapnel in his left shoulder and his right upper arm was shredded. Scared, angry, and in pain, they screamed and cussed the VC as they put out a hellish stream of deadly fire.

Charlie broke off the fight and melted back into the jungle like water into sand. I gathered the men to assess our causalities. Doc Ryan attended to Taylor and Snyder first, who moaned in agony. The blood and mud on their faces resembled a grotesque mask.

Lopez, from El Paso, had a bullet imbedded in the fleshy part of his upper thigh. At age twenty-one, he was living with his girlfriend and was the father of twin girls. Doc Ryan cut off his pant leg, applied sulfur powder for infection, and a compression bandage to stop the bleeding. I called for a medavac, but there wasn't any available. A large monsoon storm was building, so air flights would be down anyway. Knowing we'd have to walk out, Ryan decided he'd hold off morphine for Lopez as long as possible. I had the men pair up to help the wounded and started the walk back to base camp. The tough little PFC's face was a twisted grimace of pain as he struggled through the jungle with his bandaged leg.

At a river crossing, I sent two point men across to check out the depth and secure the other bank and for cover fire. After an all clear, I sent the wounded next, keeping myself and Doc Ryan back for cover fire on our side.

Big Lawrence, a six-foot-four black man, was the last to cross. Laur, as he was called, was from Georgia and had just gotten married when he was drafted. Nearing the other side, he cried out. "Ahh, leeches ... they're all over me."

"Keep moving, Laur, keep moving!" I yelled.

The big man struggled through the water weighted down by his gear and holding his rifle over his head, stumbled in near panic. He was the only one to walk into the black mass of blood suckers. On the bank, Laur fell to the ground, kicked off his boots and pants while moaning and clawing at his body, in a desperate attempt to pry off the water vampires.

Doc scraped them off with his bayonet, but it was too slow and painful. Then he tried burning them off with a Zippo lighter, which wasn't much easier. Lawrence cried out each time the fire torched his skin. The poor guy was covered in leech bites from his waist down, including his crotch.

All we could do was sit and listen to the crude surgical ordeal and try not to think of what was going on between his legs. He walked the last two miles bow-legged, carrying his pants over his shoulder. The red welts on his ebony skin, made worse by the burns, looked like huge strawberries.

All of us were covered with insect bites, open wounds, and our fatigues were muddy and torn from thorn plants. Walking through the wet sludge in muddy boots, scrubbed the flesh off of some of the men's feet. Though the going was agonizing, some found it was easier to walk in the cool mud with their boots slung around their necks.

When we finally reached the outer edge of our base camp perimeter, open sighs of relief let out as the men dropped down exhausted. I signaled for the radioman to come up.

"Big Dog One, this is Little Dog. We're at the wire. Walking wounded. We're coming in, over."

"This is Big Dog. I'll alert the guards. Welcome back."

I sat down waiting to hear the all clear from the perimeter guard posts. I didn't want us to become friendly-fire casualties. Looking back at my squad, a surge of pride went though me. They were a tough bunch of kids. Considering the weather and no air support, we all were lucky to be alive. Only determination and youthful stubbornness pulled us through.

I'm sure they were thinking the same as I was; a hot meal, hot coffee, a shower, some dry clothes, and maybe a few days' rest before the next mission. For a while at least, no more cold C-rations, stale water, and sleeping in water-filled fighting holes while trying to kill an enemy we couldn't see.

Receiving the clear to come in, I ordered the squad to saddle up. Only now did they seem to come alive, helping each other, joking with nervous laughter, glad they were safely back to camp. After seeing that the men got medical attention and arranging for hot food, I made my report to the captain.

"There was blood all around that jungle trail, but no VC bodies. Charlie dragged them off as usual. I know we zapped some of them, but I can't give you a body count. By the muzzle flashes and the sounds, I'd guess it was a small, well-armed force. But at the village, there was evidence of at least two company-sized movements in the area. A local old papasan said Boo-coo VC had been there."

Captain Ross stared at me a moment. He was thirty-five, a veteran of Korea, and a career soldier. "Let's see. You can't have a shoot out and not kill the enemy. I'd say you kicked their ass, Sergeant. Let's put down fifteen. That sound about right to you?"

I couldn't help smiling. "Whatever you think, Sir."

"I'll call for an air looksee after the rain," he said. "And how are you doing, Sergeant? You look pretty haggard."

"Not too bad. Lopez, Taylor, and Snyder will have to be medevaced out. Lawrence will be laid up for a few days with his leech wounds. Otherwise, we're good. Just need a little time."

"I didn't ask about your men. I wanna know how you're doing. You took a big hit this time. Half of your squad is out of action. It's not easy out there.

"Little tired, Captain. I hate seeing my boys shot up like that. Know what I mean? Sometimes, I can't stop my hands from shaking. My body is on fire from these bites, and I can't hold anything down." I smiled. "Otherwise, things are great."

"Yeah, this is a real fun place."

FRIGHT FLIGHT

Russian-made AK-47 machinegun rounds ripped through the skin of the Huey chopper with thuds and zings as we hovered two feet off the ground.

The last man, Robbie, jumped for the door and missed, straddling the landing skid with his groin. He screamed and fell backward. Hanson and I grabbed his arms and flack jacket and pulled him in, his legs still dangling out as we lifted off. He was still moaning and carrying on about his nuts while settling himself on the floor. We looked at each other. In spite of the danger, we couldn't keep from laughing.

Hanson was only nineteen, but we had a lot in common. He was from California, a high school football player and built like me, six foot, about a hundred ninety pounds. We become close having already gone through some action together. He liked the ocean and boats and talked of joining the Coast Guard to chase drug runners when he got home. Hanson would live to fulfill his dream.

The powerful Huey pulled forward, nose down for a few yards, and then lifted off with my six-man squad, of whom three were badly wounded. The gunner swung his M-60 and fired long bursts into the jungle below. Green ribbons of Viet Cong tracer rounds came up from the tree line toward the ship, but lucky for us they all fell short.

The chopper jerked sharply left. I was seated near the door next to the gunner; the sudden maneuver slammed me against the metal side. Blood flowed between my feet and across the floor from my three wounded men in the rear of the gunship. Ernie, the worst of the three, moaned from the sudden movement. All of the wounded were shot up with morphine, but Ernie's pain was beyond help. Parts of his chest and stomach had been blown away by a VC rocket. Ernie held in pieces of his intestines with his hand. I couldn't imagine how he was still alive.

My squad was the first to be lifted out after a five-day patrol. *Was the chopper any safer?* My gut was on fire. I was sure it was an ulcer. I could see the two pilot's mouths moving, excited, hands in frantic gestures.

I hit the gunner's leg, pointed to the front, and yelled, "What's wrong?"

He adjusted his flight helmet and listened. "It's nothing … be okay!" He yelled, and smiled reassuringly, with a thumbs up. I didn't believe him.

The flight smoothed out, but I was still nervous. We didn't seem to be high enough. The engine growled to gain altitude from the treetops and heavy foliage not far below. But I trusted the pilots. We were exhausted, filthy, and wet from the red earth of the Northern Province. I was thankful to be getting out of the killing zone.

It had rained the last three of the five days of the search and destroy mission. On our return trip to the landing zone we walked into a deadly ambush. My squad suffered three men wounded and two others killed in the platoon in the thirty-minute clash. We carried the bodies and the wounded a mile through high saw grass and thorn bushes. Our bodies and clothes were ripped open and bloody from the long hump. We waited for the rain to stop to get a medevac, all the while hunkered down in the rain and fending off sniper fire. Charlie had us pinned to the muddy ground. A small defense perimeter had been set up. Anyone rising up would be picked off.

Chopper pilots didn't like coming into a hot LZ. When the rain finally stopped, the Cong pretended to break off the fight. Gunships quickly swooped in and began taking us out. Then Charlie reappeared giving us a hot sendoff.

I felt my butt being soaked and moved to see blood running down the floor from Ernie Poss. Doc Ryan was frantically trying to stop the bleeding, but he was losing the battle. Ernie's mangled body shook, his head tilted back, eyes closed, mouth moving but nothing coming out. Robbie moved close enough to take his friend's dirty hand in both of his and held it tight. Ernie raised his head and smiled. The two were best buddies. We called them twins. Ernie, from Kansas, wouldn't see his twentieth birthday. Robbie put his face to the hand and began sobbing quietly. Hanson and I looked away.

Loud banging shocked me back to reality. Heavy automatic weapon fire ripped through the thin metal of the gunship; a sound like someone beating on a tin roof with a hammer. Bullets bounced and ricocheted about the cabin. Men ducked and held their helmets onto their heads. Some took off their flack jackets and sat on them for protection. Someone yelled he was hit, and the wounded moaned as the Huey rolled back and forth. The sound was deafening as the turbine engine screamed for more power. I looked out. We had lost altitude. Perhaps none of us would see another birthday.

Enemy rounds continued to hit the chopper as the pilots desperately tried evasion maneuvers. We were too low. The Huey must have been hit during the takeoff, making us an easy target.

The crazy young gunner stood in the open door, returning streams of deadly steel, sending empty cartridges clattering across the floor. I noticed the name Stevenson on his flight suit. With the helmet and dark eye visor, he looked like a robot, swinging the machine gun back and forth. I swore he was smiling.

A round hit Stevenson's thigh, splattering blood over me and everywhere. He cried out and fell to his knees. Bright blood gushed from an artery like a broken water main. I cut open his pant leg with my bayonet, pulled my bandage pack from the band around my helmet and wrapped it as tight as I could over the gushing wound.

While unhooking his safety harness, I shouted for Hanson to help me move Stevenson away from the door. Hanson broke open a morphine pack and jammed the needle into the mangled leg. As we began to drag him, the Huey dipped and swerved again. The G-force pulled Stevenson from our hands, and he slid screaming out the door. I jumped to grab him, but it happened so fast; he just disappeared. I was horrified. Hanson looked at me in disbelief, his eyes wide, mouth gaping. I prayed the morphine had had time to work.

An explosion rocked the ship, opening a large hole in the side. Shrapnel and wind blasted through the interior. The wounded cried out for Doc, others frantically screamed for help to keep from following Stevenson out the door. I grabbed a cargo strap on the side, and I held Hanson with my free hand.

Sharp crackling came from the pilot's cockpit. I looked up to see penetrating rounds rip through the Plexiglas. The pilot slumped in his seat, his helmet split in two pieces, blood gushed from the back of his head. With one hand the co-pilot arm wrestled with the joystick. With the other bloody gloved hand, he flipped switches and dials on the console and overhead panel, struggling for control of the shuddering Huey.

The ship nosed down, then pulled up and began a slow left turn, barely clearing the tree tops. We slipped and slid on the bloody floor, desperately hanging on to each other. Electrical smoke whirled about and the smell of burning oil was heavy. I knew we were going down. I closed my eyes and prayed to God to save these brave young men who didn't deserve to die such a horrible death. They had already suffered enough and were worthy to live long and happy lives. I no sooner said amen when the crippled chopper lifted and leveled off as if a giant hand had pushed it gently upward. Enemy machine gunfire stopped as we gradually chugged out of range of the VC gunners. I looked out and saw some familiar landmarks. We were headed for home.

With the exception of the cries from the wounded, everyone was silent. Hanson had a smile on his face.

"What's so funny?" I asked.

"Today's my birthday. For a minute I didn't think … " he stopped.

I smiled back, pulled a can of peaches from my pocket, and tossed them to him. "Happy birthday."

SNIPER'S WALTZ

Lieutenant Randy Carol and I sat on the wet ground and sipped coffee we'd just made. Randy was telling me about the letter he'd received from his wife. He was twenty-two and had a three-year-old daughter and a newborn baby boy he had never seen. Randy smiled when he said, "The wife said he looks just like me. Can you believe that?" He shook his head. "Man, I can't wait to see him."

A rush of air went past my face, then a wet sucking sound. Lieutenant Carol jerked backward. I dove to the ground, grabbed my rifle, and scanned the tree line beyond the kill zone in front of our perimeter. Nothing, no more shots, nor an attack... *it was the VC sniper.*

Captain Ross called out if anyone was hit. I crawled over to Randy. Blood oozed out of a black hole where his left eye had been; the other eye stared at a gray evening sky. I yelled for the medic and the captain, but I knew Randy was dead before he had hit the ground.

A sick feeling came over me. I wanted to cry, to scream, to crawl into a hole and stay there until this insanity was over. This was a crime of the highest order. I felt nauseated and lowered my face into the cool mud. Brain tissue and skull fragments, white like egg shells on the wet earth, lay inches from my face. When I closed my eyes, there was Randy's smile when he talked of his family. I threw up and let the tears ease out.

Captain Ross and Doc Ryan crawled over at the same time. Ross began cursing and screaming at the VC for killing his young lieutenant. "He was a good boy...you dirty bastards..." His voice broke and went low, "Bastards, dirty..." Then he quietly sobbed.

Randy had come to the platoon two months after Ross, and they became close friends. Randy was smart and eager to learn. Ross was a Korean veteran and a career officer who become his mentor. They made a good command team, and everyone in the company liked them both, which says a lot for officers.

Night fell. Choirs of nocturnal creatures begin tuning up like an amateur glee club. A cool damp fog settled over the area, bringing a reeking swamp odor. Earlier, Captain Ross had insisted on helping wrap

Lieutenant Carol's body in a poncho. Ross kneeled, touched his young friend's cheek, and gently covered the face. Reverently, we moved the body to the rear of the perimeter to the dust off area where two other casualties lay. Evacuation wouldn't come until daylight.

Doc Ryan and I lay in our shallow fighting hole in silence and studied the area to our front. Captain Ross, on hands and knees, moved up beside us.

"Sergeant," he said to me. "I have a job for you. I want you to go out there and get that son-of-a-bitchin' sniper. He's had us pinned to the ground for ten hours now. I can't risk sending out a patrol; it could be a trap. One man might move around and locate that bastard."

"I'm no sniper, why me?"

"You're the best shot."

"But we don't have a snipe rifle or a scope. I'd need at least an M-14 for a distance shot," I said.

"I don't give a damm about all that. I want him dead. Use your bayonet if you have too. Take what you need. You move out at 0400, find a place, and wait until dawn. At precisely 0600, I'll set up a dummy target to draw his fire, and hopefully, you'll be able to spot him. Got it?"

I nodded yes. I got it all right, but I didn't like it. I wanted Carol's death revenged as much as anyone but I didn't dream I'd be the one called upon to do it. The thought of going out there in the black night terrified me. I'd come to hate the dark, since most of the fighting came when the sun went down, or during a miserable rain, or fog. But the captain had chosen me and I didn't want to let him down ... besides, it was an order, not a choice.

My M-16 was effective up to 400 meters, but closer would be better. I put a can of C-rations in my pocket, two canteens of water, two bandages, two clips of thirty rounds each, my bayonet, binoculars, and two .45 pistols. It might come to a close-quarter fight. I might only get one chance at him, but if he spotted me first, it would be over.

Instead of a helmet, I wore my jungle soft hat, which made less of an outline in the bush. I blackened my face and all exposed skin areas and tied my camo bandana about my neck. Returning to my fighting hole, I told Doc Ryan what was happening and to give me a wake-up at three forty-five.

"Hope you don't need this," he said, and handed me a morphine pack and a green smoke grenade. "But just in case. If you're unable to make it back, pull this. We'll come find you." I thanked him and patted his shoulder.

At four I found the captain and told him I was ready. Alert the perimeter posts.

He laid his hand on my shoulder. "Good luck, Sergeant. I'll have the coffee on."

Approaching the perimeter line next to two soldiers, I whispered, "Man going out." I crouched low and moved out into the blackness. The nighttime hum of insects was coupled with whispers of men behind me saying, "Man going out ... man going out." As the words faded away, it was like entering a black vacuum where I was to fight the war alone.

After skirting around the kill zone beyond our perimeter, it was almost impossible to see anything in the dark. I moved another hundred yards until I found a tree and a clump of bushes. It was good concealment and an excellent position when daylight came. The sniper was probably in a tree or on one of the large abandoned anthills within three to five hundred meters of the camp. With a good rifle and scope, he could be even further out.

I hunkered down, my back against the tree. A cold breeze whipped the trees, bushes, and elephant grass like spooks in *Sleepy Hollow*. I checked my ammo clip, flipped on semi-automatic. Firing too many rounds would give my position away.

I rested my eyes. Suddenly the sniper was standing over me, smiling, his rifle pointed at my head. I jolted awake and wondered if I had cried out ... the image was so real. I hurt from fear, and my heart was beating in my ears. I didn't dare relax again.

Dawn came. A dark, ominous sky unveiled and a breeze carried the smell of wet earth. I rolled up on my knees and surveyed the vicinity: large open fields of tall grass, some trees, and a couple of five-foot abandoned anthills.

At six, I looked back at our perimeter on the high ground and saw the top of the dummy target helmet move about. With the field glasses, I swept the area again with the binoculars, particularly the trees, hoping he'd take the shot. The timing couldn't have been more perfect. There was a poof of rifle smoke, the muffled sound of a silencer, and then the ping of a direct hit through the helmet. *He's in the Y of a tree*, about a hundred meters to my left, rifle with scope resting on a branch.

I braced my M-16 against the tree, took a deep breath, took aim at the figure, and squeezed off two rapid shots. Quickly I lowered the rifle and looked through the binoculars. The tree was empty. Had I got him? I scanned all around, but I couldn't see a body. He could be hidden by the grass. I had to find him.

I began to crawl, not wanting to become his target or be fired upon by my own men. Within minutes I was under the tree. Nobody. There was blood on the trunk and the ground … he was hit but managed to escape. I leaned against the tree to see which direction he had gone.

A muffled pop kicked up dirt beside me. I rolled to the ground and crawled into the four-foot high grass and lay still, listening, straining to see something. I had to move fast, find another hiding place, and pray that I saw him first.

Thunder rolled like kettle drums; it grew darker, and rain began to fall. I looked through the binoculars and found another tree about thirty meters ahead. No sniper. I crawled through the mud, pulling myself with the grass.

By the time I reached the small clearing around the tree, I was breathing hard. After catching my breath, I eased up and took a cautious look through the binoculars.

To my horror, he was on an anthill not more than fifty meters away looking directly at me through his scope. He fired; the round hit my rifle, shattering it in pieces, stinging my hand. Stunned and dazed, I fell to the ground. Again, I had to act quickly. He would be coming to confirm his kill or finish me off

I pulled my .45 and crawled back into the tall grass fast as possible, trying not to make noise. But I hadn't gone more then ten feet when I heard something behind me ... was it the rain, legs brushing the grass? I rolled over, looked behind me, listened. The swishing sound came closer, faster. Thoughts raced through my head ... maybe he wouldn't see me covered with mud ... play dead or unarmed. I slid the .45 under my hip.

Out of the mist came a staggering figure, rifle hanging at his side. I held my breath. He stood before me breathing hard the unsteady AK-47 now pointed at my head. His face was wet, his black hair slicked down from the rain. The tan NVA uniform was covered with blood, oozing from his left shoulder and side; his eyelids were heavy, he swayed, but he was still alert. I had hit him with both shots, and he had lost a lot of blood while moving around. He was not only a good marksman, but a tough, veteran soldier. I felt an odd feeling of respect ... then I shuddered with fear.

Suddenly, the sniper sank to his knees, the rifle still pointed at me. I knew he was quite capable of pulling the trigger any moment.

He said. "You numba one G.I. Numba one shot."

I didn't know what to say except: "You number one too, Charlie. Good shot."

Yellow teeth beamed in a twisted, painful smile. He bowed his head in acceptance of being honored. The blast from my .45 was loud as the round punched a small hole through the top of his forehead, blowing his brains and skull matter out the back of his head. A small stream of blood ran from the hole in front. The sniper snapped over backward like an empty sack.

"From this range, Charlie, it's hard to miss."

I dragged his rifle to me, a gift for the captain, then laid back, took a deep breath, and let it out. I felt completely drained. After a few moments, I got to my knees, holstered the .45, and looked toward our perimeter. I felt the cool rain on my face. I searched the tree line for any VC movement; there was none, only tree branches swaying slowly in the breezy rain like a crowd waving good-bye. I crouched low and moved swiftly through the wet grass.

Our perimeter came into view. Barely visible were the camo-covered helmets and mounds of dirt; I squatted down to catch my breath. My clothes were soaking wet, and I shuddered with a chill. I called just loud enough for the defense line to hear me. "American soldier coming in ... American coming in."

A voice called back, "Come on in ... *American sniper coming in ...*"

I stood up and walked slowly toward the voice and smelled the aroma of fresh brewed coffee.

CHILDREN OF WAR

Whether on patrol in Saigon or passing through a village with a convoy, it's the children I noticed first. Small boys and girls would run along beside the vehicles shouting, "You got gum, GI? You have chocolet for me? Have cigalet, Joe?" They crowded around, dirty faces, grubby little hands reaching out. Some wore filthy, tattered clothes, while others had on white shirt and blue bottoms of a school uniform. No child was opposed to begging. They touched my fatigues. Fascinated by the hair on my arms, they pull it lightly grinning up at me. "You numba one, GI." The attention is like that of a celebrity, the American hero come to save their country. They are cheerful and happy we are there. Some soldiers carried extra C-rations just for the children.

Village children, "Gimmy gum G.I."

One sad-eyed little girl about eight years old, small for her age, held a diapered baby on her hip; probably a sibling, its nose running. I wondered about the parents. In many cases, I learned that the parents were dead or serving with the Viet Cong, or the NVA, North Vietnamese Army, either by choice or unwillingly. This leaves the little girl to raise the family. The teenage boys and girls were abducted into the armies. It wouldn't be unusual to come face-to-face with a fifteen-year-old boy or girl carrying an AK-47 on the battlefield. The Vietnamese are little people and you never really knew if you were fighting kids or men. There was no basketball or Barbie doll for these kids.

The children left me with mixed emotions. But it was the little kids that really captured my heart and made me laugh. They would do anything to grab your attention from the other kids. They'd sing and giggle, clap their hands and dance. One little guy was quite the dancer, swinging his arms, little bandy legs kicking high. "Look me, GI. Give me gum, give me candy!" he'd laugh and shout.

Nearly all the kids smoke, as young as five and six years of age. Some could blow smoke rings to impress us for more handouts. A cute little girl made a quarter disappear. Not very well, but give her a coin and it's gone. The begging group is like a three-ring circus, all vying for an audience.

When we searched a village and found VC weapons, ammo, explosives, and rice storages, it's either a VC village or sympathizers that aid and abet the Cong. We would burn the village and destroy the rice storages so the VC could not use it. The children have been known to set off grenades or explosives in a group of GIs, killing them or blowing off an arm or leg. The charity changes when the guy next to me has his face blown off and splatters me with blood. I wanted to kill every gook in sight and get the hell out of there. *After that, I'd ignore the children's dilemma and give them nothing. Or just toss candy bars and gum at them like animals in a zoo.* I can't blame them, but the rage and anger is all consuming, and it's all I can do. It can drive you crazy if you let it. Daily, our principles and sanity are tested.

Villagers appeared to be happy and content; their family farm life carries on as it has for centuries. Most are friendly and humble, willing to do whatever they can for the Americans; others stare with fear and hatred in their eyes. The farmers wore the typical black silk or cotton pajama clothing, but it is also the unwritten uniform code for the VC gorillas that roam the jungle. One can't tell who the real enemy is … farmer by day, Viet Cong by night. The psychological affect was brutal. Anyone wearing black was a potential threat, reasons for alarm and anxiety.

In the city of Saigon, one tough little streetwise guy spoke excellent English, he was a hustler who was homeless; he survived on his wits and charm. Soldiers gave him a nickname like Spanky of Our Gang or Mugsy of the Bowery Boys. This kid could get anything you want or point you in the right direction. "You want a bottle of booze, some dope? How about some weed?" Some men took him up on the offers.

I was surprised one day when he quietly asked me, "MP, you want a handgun? I can get. What about a VC flag?" The flag was one item the troops really wanted for a war souvenir. The red and blue flags with a yellow star in the middle, along with NVA officer's swords, could be found on the battlefield, but they were sparse. As for weapons, we had all we needed from our own dead and wounded, plus many taken from the enemy. But for the soldier stuck behind a desk, a VC flag, pistol, or an NVA officer's sword was the absolute trophy. I wondered where Spanky got the flags. Was he friendly with the Viet Cong too? Or were the flags being made in the city, just for souvenirs.

When asked where he learned English, Spanky says, "You man," meaning the GIs. When asked about his home and parents, he'll say, "No mama'san, no papa'san, VC fin'ee." He runs a finger across his throat, meaning they were killed. True or not, the grotesque gesture is the quickest way to your heart. Likely he doesn't know his parents and probably lives in an orphanage or on the streets.

Many of the kids are homeless. Some have families living in city apartments or a short distant from downtown. There's another group called the Boat People. They live on boats along the Saigon River, having never lived on land. Everything that is done in a home is done on the small boats such as cooking and washing clothes over the edge. If it's hot and humid, the children think nothing of jumping into the filthy water to cool off and play. When patrolling the river streets, some of these kids turn out with a gift for the MPs, offering us dried, smelly fish and saying, "Good, you eat," with a big smile. We kindly refuse, give them candy or something, and move on.

The Saigon River boat people, where many of the children lived.

Most children are truly desperate and grateful for what we give them. But there's that one percent who have but one mission … that is to kill us … to blow us to hell with a hand grenade or plastic explosive in a bag or basket. We don't learn this until it's too late. Sometimes the enemy is a child with a happy face and his hand out.

Vietnamese village – cong or friendly?

AFTERNOON BARBECUE

Convoy coming into Saigon.

When our company was reassigned to the city of
Saigon as a security force, the men were overjoyed.
After eight months in the dangerous bush or convoys
on dirt roads, Saigon sound like a Disneyland vacation. The night before departure, the men shaved

and laid out their cleanest fatigues. Excited chatter filled with talk of booze, broads, and beds. No more Charlie, at least not so close.

The convoy was a long line of trucks and jeeps mounted with .50-caliber machine guns and other vehicles carrying our supplies. My squad was in high spirits when the city skyline came into view with a large arching bridge crossing the Saigon River. But the mood quickly turned foul when we pulled onto the streets, where huge mounds of garbage lined the curbs; starving dogs, cats, and even people rooted through the heaps for food. Old men and women squatted on the sidewalks eating things that looked raw and ugly. Plucked chickens and gutted pigs covered with flies hung in meat market windows. The air was thick with smells from open fires and boiling pots along the sidewalks. Like New York vendors, they were cooking and selling food. But unlike the Big Apple's hot dogs and warm pretzel hawkers, these were plucked ducks, parts of pig, and a dozen other unidentifiable pieces of meat. Some looked like beef jerky, though I'm sure it wasn't. On the plus side, there were nice-looking fresh fruit and vegetables on display. Ripe papaya, mangos, and bananas looked delicious. But ... we had been warned not to eat from the street vendors. The VC would enlist and reward the vendors that poisoned unsuspecting GIs. There had been cases where a soldier died an agonizing death within hours of eating poisoned food.

Garbage piles in Saigon.

A walk down the street opened up a whole new culture where the strangest morsels were considered delicacies. An old lady squatted on her haunches, holding something up to me in her hand. A closer look revealed that it was a featherless chick still in a cracked shell. In broken English the woman, with dark skin and age-lined face, said, *No feathers numba one, you eat, you like … have feather numba ten …* I almost lost my cookies right there on the street.

Coming through the streets of Saigon.

While patrolling in our machine gun jeep, a group of children ahead of us were dancing and chanting something in their sing song language. We stopped to see what the commotion was about. They were chanting, "*Con'chaw (dog)* numba one chop-chop." The group carried an animal tied by its legs to a long pole held between two boys. It was a dog, dead and skinned, and being transported somewhere to be hung over an open fire and cooked to order. It was unsettling to see how happy these boys and girls were to be eating a dog.

There were skinny dogs and cats everywhere, but I guessed there was a specific breed of animal with more meat considered more desirable for dinner. In the upper-class neighborhoods, which the French had settled back in the 1950s, many owned thor-

oughbred dogs as pets. Fine, healthy canine speci-
mens were costly. Chances are the kids would slip
over into the well-to-do neighborhoods and collect
a nice dog or two.

Suburb of Saigon.

Vietnamese taxi – cycle'lo boy.

Later, when my tour of duty was over, I returned to California. When Saigon and South Vietnam finally fell to the North Vietnam Army, the United States gladly welcomed in thousands of Vietnamese refugees. Hundreds settled in the San Francisco area. It wasn't long before residents in the neighborhood began missing their dogs. It took only a short time to discover the Vietnamese families were taking the pets for an afternoon barbecue dinner. Though I'm sure they didn't parade down the street with a fine-looking poodle hanging from a pole.

THE RIVER

The Saigon River was like an interstate highway with boats and ships of all shapes and sizes moving up and down the watery blacktop. But the Viet Cong liked using the river to disrupt shipping of supplies and the movement of American and Vietnamese troops.

Charlie would try to destroy bridges by floating rafts downriver loaded with explosives camouflaged in trees or bushes, set off by remote control. A mile upriver from the Saigon Bridge, the Vietnamese Army set up checkpoints and outposts to monitor suspicious things floating by.

Army Republic of Vietnam outpost on the river.

Patrolling the river.

The captain would send out patrols to help with securing the river bridges. A few of us would line up along the river bank, firing rifles or grenade launchers at anything that looked out of place. Suddenly there would be a loud, ground-shaking, mind-numbing explosion that rocked our senses. We all jumped, arms and rifles flailing in the air, cheering like kids at a football game. What a thrill and exhilaration seeing the water and debris flying high in the sky. We had succeeded again. My ears rang and I couldn't hear anything for five minutes.

One time Charlie actually rode the raft in order to detonate the explosives at the precise moment and position under the bridge. But something went horribly wrong for the poor guy. For some reason, the bomb detonated itself before reaching its target, blowing him apart.

ARVN Patrol.

Bridge sabotaged by the VC.

A CHRISTMAS TREE
IN VIETNAM

Our dayroom had a bar, pool table, tables, chairs, a radio, and cassette player. The old six-story hotel in Saigon was the home of my MP company. When not patrolling the streets, some of our off-duty time was spent there drinking beer, listening to music from cassettes family sent, waiting for the next patrol. We also received mail call there.

One day, PFC William "Willie" Harris got a letter from his mother. "Hey, my mom is sending us a Christmas tree to put in here, one of those aluminum things with all the decorations. It'll be here before Christmas. We just have to put it together."

No one, including me, was excited at the news except Willie. He kept looking at the letter as if for the first time, with a smile on his face. Willie was short and thin, mild mannered, and wore glasses.

When there was no response, I told him it would be nice having a tree. I had a feeling Christmas could be a real downer here. Our company had already lost three men during an attack on another military hotel. We could use some Christmas sprit.

Two weeks later, Willie's package arrived. The box looked like it had had a rough trip. "It's here, the Christmas tree!" he shouted.

A package, regardless of who received one, was always a point of interest. Sometimes, it meant homemade cookies or candy to be shared, music cassettes, or maybe a photo of a girl.

A few of us gathered around as Willie tore into the box. When it was open we stared at the contents, the disassembled tree, and all the decorations were in a million pieces. We looked at each other, then at Willie, who stared in silence. It went quiet. No one knew what to say. Gradually, everyone moved away, some said "nice tree," or "very cool." But Willie stood looking at the mess.

My heart went out to him. I knew how much he was looking forward to having the tree for the dayroom. He was eighteen and an only child. But he came from a large family with many cousins, aunts, and uncles. Willie often talked of family holidays, especially Christmas, and how they all gathered around a tree at their grandmother's.

I put my hand on his shoulder. "It was very thoughtful of your mother. Thank her anyway...for all of us."

As I started to turn away, tears had swelled in Willie's eyes, his lower lip quivered. He lowered his head and quietly wept. Allen, the bartender, gave him a beer, saying it was on the house. Willie sat at a table alone.

I went back to the box. Even the chocolate chip cookies were in crumbs. It troubled me a great deal, and I knew it had affected the other men as well. Hopelessness and sorrow hung in the room for what was to be an uplifting event.

It was three days before Christmas. We couldn't let this get us down. I began pulling out the pieces, straightening the stems and placing them into the holes in the metal, round trunk. One of the young boys came over, and began doing the same thing...then another, and another.

The activity caught Willie's attention, and he came to see what was going on. When the tree was complete, it was six feet tall. Most of the branches were bent and naked of the aluminum pine bush. It looked pretty sad, like a Charlie Brown Christmas tree.

One of the guys took off his brass belt buckle and fixed it onto a branch. Bartender Allen brought out a box of red and white straws, twisted them together, and they looked like candy canes. He placed the straws on the branches, along with some little cocktail umbrellas.

That did it. Everyone began finding little things for the tree, a bent spoon and fork, a key chain, a P-38 can opener, sunglasses, and any objects we could find for decorations. Allen became even more creative, stringing together green and red pimento olives that resembled Christmas lights. Even the broken decorations were used. The hooks had bright pieces of colored glass left hanging, adding lots of shiny colors.

Someone got the bell used for happy hour call, began ringing it, and started singing "Jingle Bells." Others joined in another song, "Deck the Halls with Poison Ivy." It became a festive occasion.

A couple of soldiers had received candy and cookies for Christmas. They placed them around the tree. Finished, we stood back and admired our work. It was a great-looking tree. Maybe the best I'd ever seen.

You should have seen Willie's face: a big grin, eyes wide with excitement. He moved to the tree and studied it carefully. Then something unexpected happened. His eyes began to tear. He tried to speak, but only low sounds came out…then finally, the words to "Silent Night." It grew quiet like a church. One by one, others joined in until the whole room was softly singing the beautiful, touching Christmas carol. Visions of home and family must have floated in their head, for tears were now being shed by almost everyone. I felt something wet roll down my cheek.

To this day, it's the best Christmas I can remember, and the memory still brings a lump to my throat.

THE GREEN BAG

It was early morning but still dark. My partner and I were near the end of our midnight patrol in Saigon when gunfire erupted two blocks away. We rushed to the sound. Rounding the corner in our machine gun jeep, I slammed on the brakes when we came face-to-face with the Viet Cong in the middle of the street. Half a dozen VC were behind a car and a small truck, attacking the American officer's military hotel. Red and green tracer rounds ricocheted off walls, bounced, and twirled on the street like Crazy Joes or Piccolo Pete fireworks.

Orange, red, and yellow flashes glistened off the windows. Luminous green rounds slammed into the front of our jeep, bouncing off the hood over our heads; some smashed into the steel plating, rocking the vehicle. I felt zings of hot air pass my head as we hunkered down behind the armored-plated shields protecting us. From the driver's seat I fired my M-16, emptying magazine after magazine. Sergeant Melville let loose a shower of steel from his M-60 machine gun. Hot shell casings filled the space between us.

I saw another MP jeep just a few yards away, the two men slumped in their seats riddled with bullets. Caught in the ambush, they never had a chance.

Another MP and a local policeman returned fire from their bunker in front of the hotel entrance. One of the Cong jumped into the small truck and drove it toward the building. He crashed the vehicle into the front doors, jumped out, and within seconds the hotel and the two men disappeared in a horrific ball of fire and a column of smoke. The ground rocked; the sound was ear busting.

Showers of metal and debris rained down. Dust, smoke, and rubble rolled over us like monsoon rain. We coughed and choked on the air thick with sulfate and billowing waste. As the smoke cleared, ash floated down from a dawning, yellow sky. Melville and I walked around looking for an officer and assisted with the causalities. The front of the hotel had been completely blown away by the car bomb. The exposed rooms stood open like the catacombs of death. Bloody people wandered around moaning, holding their heads, dazed, amid the smoke and rubble. More MPs, ambulances, fire trucks, and local policemen arrived.

In the ambushed jeep, a young lieutenant and his driver were torn apart, their bodies twisted and bloody from head to foot. I turned away just in time to throw up. I wandered over to the VC car perforated with hundreds of bullet holes. Five small bodies lay behind the vehicle still smoldering from the burning tracer rounds, their bodies wrinkled in death. I felt nothing but hatred for them.

Melville was talking to a captain at the hotel when I came up. Two men were putting the body of the dead MP into a green plastic bag. I moved closer. The bag had two handles at each end. It was about seven feet long with the word *head* stenciled in black on one end. Blood flowed from the open bag as a soldier carefully placed the dead man's hands across his chest. On one wrist was a leather, beaded bracelet.

My knees gave way and I sank to the ground. It was Jerry Pederson, my friend from the indoctrinations when we arrived in Vietnam. His plans and dream of marrying his girlfriend would never happen.

STAR OVER SAIGON

A hard, monsoon rain fell, the night pitch black. The rain rolled off our helmets onto the rubber ponchos, chilling our bodies. It was after curfew, and except for the huge rats, whose red eyes shined in the dark, the streets were deserted. The cat-sized rodents scurried in and out of large piles of garbage that stunk like a septic tank.

My driver, PFC Bobby Franks, and I were in an open jeep moving slowly down a quiet street in Saigon. We were one of many military police patrols roaming the city to guard against VC attacks on American installations. Intelligence warned of a possible major offensive that would be launched over the holidays.

Our patrol jeep.

My nerves were tattered. I spooked at every shadow, every sound, knowing death could be waiting in the darkness or around the next corner. When the radio cracked to life, we both jumped. "This is Waco, all patrol units switch to channel two." Channel two was reserved for security messages or combat information. It usually meant trouble.

I told PFC Franks to pull over and change the channel. Then I reinspected the M-60 machine gun mounted to the floor in front of me, examining the breach, the ammo belt, and then swinging the weapon from side to side. It was ready.

The radio came on again, casting a red glow across Bobby's young face.

A voice spoke, "This is Waco. All units stand by."

What are we in for now? I touched the cold weapon, searching for comfort and security. I was twenty-six years old, but I felt much older and worn out. The months of combat and stress had taken their toll. Thinking of home and family made me wonder if I would leave this horrible place alive; or if I would ever find the woman of my dreams and have a family again. I shook off the thought.

Bobby was eighteen or nineteen, as were most of the soldiers over there. I never thought of him as a kid, but as another brave soldier. His hands shook, fear and anxiety obvious in his pale eyes. This was no place for boys or men; it was a place of death and destruction, of terror and horror.

The radio came on again. We were ready. "Waco control to all units." A pause, then, "Merry Christmas. And may God bless and protect us all. Continue patrol, Waco out."

We looked at each other. I checked my watch. It was one minute past midnight, December 25.

"My gosh, Sarge. I completely forgot."

"Yeah, me too." Suddenly I felt lonely and empty.

"We shouldn't be here, Sarge," Bobby said, his eyes tearing. "We should be home, not here in this stinking hellhole. We should be home with our families."

A disturbing buildup of fear, the anticipated danger, and then the unexpected reprieve by the holy event was more than Bobby could handle. I sensed that from somewhere deep in his soul something let go, releasing uncontrollable, forgotten feelings, and he broke down and cried unashamedly.

I turned away, not wanting to embarrass the young man. But the moment had overcome me too, unearthing emotions that could no longer be held in check, and I too began to silently weep.

Suddenly, the rain stopped, leaving only the sounds of dripping water and fast moving currants pushing garbage down the gutters.

After a moment Bobby said, "You know, Sarge, there hasn't been a shot fired all night."

I looked up and scanned around as if I might find the answer. Abruptly, the night sky lit up, and for a second it looked like a flare, which was usually followed by an attack. This is it, what we had been expecting all along.

It wasn't a flare at all, but the brightest star I had ever seen breaking through the cloud cover. The street was as bright as day.

Gone were the feelings that had consumed me just minutes before, replaced with an inner peace and comfort I had never before known. No longer did I feel alone or abandoned, but warm and safe, as if someone was holding me. We stared at the brilliant star, unable to turn away.

"Happy birthday, Jesus. And thank you for loving me. Amen," I said.

"What did you say, Sarge?"

"Nothing, just thinking out loud."

"Merry Christmas, Sergeant." He was smiling and there was calmness on his face.

"Merry Christmas, Franks. We're sitting ducks here. Let's get moving before someone decides to take a shot at us." We chuckled.

Bobby put the jeep in gear and we moved slowly down the quiet street. It was Christmas in Saigon.

THE GRAVEYARD

Our squad had been assigned to secure an old pagoda to be used for an observation post on the outskirts of Saigon. An orange sun slipped down behind the jungle, and a wet fog floated in. We were walking in single file passing an old cemetery when the Viet Cong opened up on us. We found cover, and a short but furious firefight ensued. The still of the night erupted into a laser and sound show as tracer rounds zinged and ricocheted everywhere as we fired at anything that moved. We fought them back into the nearby graveyard. The VC disappeared among the headstones.

Just inside the large iron gates, squad leader Sergeant Mays quietly gave hand signals for us to spread out. I walked slowly, bent low, straining to see through the dense fog. It was very quiet. Charlie was waiting for us. From time to time, large headstones appeared out of the mist.

Suddenly there was a noise to my right and in front of me. I froze. The sound of soft footsteps came from behind one of the large monuments. Slowly I raised my M-16. My finger shook as it moved to the trigger. I waited for a clear shot. A shadowy figure, barely visible through the fog, moved to the edge of the monument and stopped. I couldn't see clearly but could make out the ghostlike movement. Then the shadow moved from behind the monument and I saw the round outline of an American helmet. It was one of my guys, a friend from California that I almost shot. I let out the breath I'd been holding.

My hands shook, sweat ran down my forehead, and my insides quivered. I continued with calculated steps.

Suddenly I felt the ground grow soft under my feet. Before I could do anything to help myself, the earth gave way and I fell down to my armpits, my weapon landing a few feet away. Desperately I hung on by my outstretched arms, unable to move up or down. I had fallen into a grave.

I hung there helpless. There was nothing I could do but wait and pray that Charlie didn't find me first. What would the Viet Cong do if they found me? Cut off my head? Shoot me? The thought was horrifying, and it seemed to have gotten darker. I could hear water dripping, night birds, and the earth smelled like a sewer. My arms began to tire.

It seemed like hours waiting for my men to come looking for me. No shots had been fired since we entered the graveyard. Had I been left behind? How long could I hold on? I didn't know which frightened me more, falling completely into the grave or the possibility of being killed or captured. Whenever I tried to move, I slipped a little deeper and swore something tugged at my foot.

Finally, I managed to find one wall and got a foothold, but I still couldn't get out. Then there were whispers. Someone was coming. Who? I didn't move, wishing I could disappear. Should I call out? My mouth was dry. Suddenly, out of the thick fog, two figures appeared, phantomlike, moving toward me. My God, who were they? They came closer, their weapons hanging low. What were they, Viet Cong...American? They looked ghostly. I could hear my heart pounding. Sweat burned my eyes.

Suddenly there was laughter, American voices. "Well, look what we have here! A grave robber," one of my men said. I laughed with them as they pulled me from the muddy hole. The Viet Cong had slipped out the back of the graveyard.

Now whenever I pass a cemetery, I smile and then shudder at the memory.

CHECK, PLEASE

Oh crap, I had to buy again. I thought as I raked in another sizeable pot of cash from the poker table. Doc Ryan, Leonard, and I had a deal that whoever won at poker would pay for dinner. We spend most of our spare time at a never ending poker game in our hotel billet. Players would come and go as duty required, but the game never stopped, a marathon, year-long poker game. That should be in the Guinness World Book. Ryan and Leonard were decent players, but I'd been playing poker since a teen and my skills were quite honed. The game was seven-card-stud. Texas Hold'em wasn't popular at that time.

"Man, you're the luckiest son'bitch I ever saw," Leonard said in his southern accent. He refused to accept that I was just a good player. But Doc knew it and played hard against me whenever he could. He had only begun playing poker in college and was a serious player, attacking the game like his medical studies.

Doc Ryan, another California boy was two years into UCLA medical school when he was drafted. He probably could have gotten a deferment but he didn't try. He actually relished being a combat medic. *Much better training*, he always said.

Leonard, on the other hand, was bitter. Only eighteen and black, he had lived close to poverty in Georgia and loved his new job as an apprentice auto mechanic when Uncle Sam called. His objective was simple: get back home alive and work.

We usually ate at the Chicago Club, within walking distance from our military police company's billet. Our headquarters was an ancient, six-story building in a district of Saigon. The average-sized hotel rooms were crammed with up to seven men and combat gear.

The Chicago Club was an MP hangout, an upscale bar and restaurant built by the French in the 1950s. It was also frequented by foreign civilians, journalists, a few local professionals, and American company employees who worked in Saigon. After changing into civilian clothes, we met in front of our hotel and headed down the sidewalk to the restaurant.

In 1967 a Saigon street could be as deadly as a jungle trail. The Viet Cong could be anyone; a woman on a bike, a kid with a hand grenade, a sniper on a rooftop or in an alley. A package could be a street-side bomb. A passing car might be carrying VC with machine guns. The Viet Cong had a bounty for killing MPs, which made us a special target.

Downtown Saigon.

At the Chicago Club, we took a table with our backs to the wall, facing the door and window. I felt the hard, steel Beretta in the small of my back when I sat down. Doc and Leonard also carried side arms. It wasn't safe for MPs in public, even dressed in our street clothes; the Viet Cong spies knew who we were.

I liked the steak, though the toothy manager called it sirloin or prime cut. We all knew it was water buffalo, pounded until tender, spiced until delicious, and garnished until presentable. The potatoes, vegetables, and rice were fresh from the fields and all were excellent.

I was only two bites into my prime cut when two Vietnamese men busted through the door brandishing rifles. I yelled, "Viet Cong!" The once pleasant hum of a dining room turned into a deafening roar of machine gunfire. AK-47 rounds ripped through bodies, tables, floors, and walls, sending splinters of wood and glass in every direction.

Table and chairs were overturned as everyone dove for cover. Dishes crashed and people screamed like a scene from a movie, only this was real. We returned fire from behind the table, our handguns adding only a popping noise to the mayhem. The automatic weapons discharged clouds of gunpowder smoke and sulfur stink. Hot, empty cartridges bounced on the floor.

A single AK round tore through the table and grazed the side of Leonard's head. Blood splattered my face as he screamed and fell backward. His finger still clutched on the trigger, sending two shots into the air.

My ten-round Italian Beretta was empty in seconds, but before I could grab another clip, the shooting stopped and the VC vanished as quickly as they had appeared.

I looked at Leonard sitting on the floor, holding his head, moaning. The white bone of his skull showed through the opened scalp. Doc quickly pushed the table aside and grabbed a nearby waiter's towel and placed it on Leonard's head. Only minutes earlier, we were all laughing, the war a long way off. This was the one place we had felt safe. But there are no boundaries in war, only warzones.

Yelling in panic and calling for help, terror-stricken patrons and Vietnamese employees ran frantically about the smoky diner. Bodies lay in pools of blood on the floor. Outside, a Vietnamese ambulance and MP jeeps arrived. We helped Leonard to his feet, braced him between us, and stepped over the destruction on our way to the door.

As we put him in the ambulance, he said, "I'll be back to get those bastards."

A young male waiter, with an ugly wound in his shoulder looked at us.

"MP okay?" he said.

"Yeah, number one," I answered.

"VC numba ten," he said.

"You got that right pal … check, please."

SHE'S NO LADY

During the day, our MP company patrolled Saigon in open jeeps. The Vietnamese government didn't want automatic weapons going off in a crowd during the day. But at night, the jeeps were mounted with an M-60 machine gun, steel plating, and sandbags. After a night curfew, only our patrols, Vietnamese police, and ARVN soldiers were on the deserted streets.

Daytime was curb-to-curb of small cars, bicycles, cycle'lows (pedal taxi), and pushcarts. Pedestrians took what space was left. In the heavy traffic we traveled five to ten miles per hour. Air pollution was immense. Smoke and exhaust fumes bellowed from vehicles and motorbikes, the stink from sidewalk food vendors was sickening, and the smell of dead animals was enough to make you toss your cookies.

I was a Spec 4 and a squad leader. My driver that day was nineteen-year-old PFC Willard from Arkansas. Sometimes we received calls to assist our foot patrols when off-duty GIs got into trouble in the Saigon bars, like a drunken brawl. Or a GI felt cheated by a bartender or one of the many bargirls. We also checked guard posts at American buildings and installations. Should they be attacked, we were to race to their aid.

At a stop sign, I noticed an attractive young Vietnamese woman standing on the sidewalk with her bicycle. She wore the typical "Aot-Than," white and olive garb down to her feet. Her hair was jet-black, long, and straight, the sides pinned back with a barrette.

She smiled and I politely smiled back. We pulled away. A few minutes later, we stopped again. To my surprise, the young girl on her bike was standing next to me. She smiled; I nodded.

Blocks later, the young lady was on the other side, smiling at Willard. Something slithered up my spine, something scary, suspicious, and treacherous. Adrenaline shot out warning signals. I fingered my M-16, watching until she disappeared into the crowd.

"Hey, Sarge, see that gal? Pretty nice for a slope, huh?" he said.

"She's okay. Keep your eyes on the road." I had already seen how calloused these people could be toward the Americans. You didn't know who you could trust no matter how innocent or pretty they may look. An old man, a little kid and yes, even a beautiful woman could kill you just as fast as the Viet Cong, and sometimes they did.

We moved sluggishly through traffic. I searched every building, windows, rooftops, and alleyways. It was hot and muggy. My eyes were red and burning from the pollution. My neck hurt from looking up.

From another intersection we slowly took off. I caught movement from the corner of my eye, an arm swung toward the vehicle ... the clank of metal on metal. I knew immediately what it was.

I turned to see that same young lady peel off onto a side street, standing up, pumping hard. I looked in the back floorboard. It was a live Viet Cong potato-masher-type grenade.

"Grenade! Get out!" I yelled and pushed hard on Willard's shoulder, sending him from his seat. I did a tuck and roll onto the street, landing hard on the smelly asphalt.

Willard looked at me in panic, and then we watched the jeep creep down the street in low gear. I leaped up, yelled, and waved for people to move away from the jeep, but most looked at me like I was a crazy man. I shouted to Willard to stay down and then hit the street myself, trying to implant myself into the asphalt.

The explosion from the jeep was earsplitting as it hit the curb and stopped. I held my helmet down with my hands, feeling the concussion vibrate through the street under me. Metal and shrapnel rained down on us. Hot fragments burned through my fatigues to my skin.

Quickly I jumped up and shook myself off. My ears rang, and there was the smell of sulfur and hot metal in the air. There were bodies around the jeep, some moving, some still, voices of panic, moans of pain, blood flowing on the street.

It was a heart-wrenching scene; two of the victims were little girls, their small bodies torn and bleeding.

I ran to the jeep to check the radio, but it was mangled. I tried it anyway; no good. The explosion was loud and could be heard for blocks. Other MP patrols and Vietnamese police would arrive any minute.

I told Willard to help the victims. His eyes wide with terror and confusion, but he reacted quickly. I grabbed the first aid kit from the smoking vehicle and began doing the same. In minutes the police and ambulances arrived, along with my duty officer, a young captain. I gave him a quick report.

We soon learned this was the beginning of the infamous Tet Offensive with the attack on Saigon and other cities throughout the southern country. The VC didn't care who they killed as long as they got Americans in the process. There was no regard for their own people, making me hate them even more. I could not wait to get one of them in the sight of my M-16.

SWEET REVENGE

The Tet Offensive had begun, and the attack on Saigon was in full swing. The day after the strike on the American Embassy that killed several military policemen and fifteen Viet Cong, the fight had overflowed into running street battles.

As we patrolled the city streets in our machine gun jeep, chills ping-ponged around my body from a cold rain. Rounding a corner, two VC, one with an AK-47, crossed the street in front of us. Seeing us, the one fired aimlessly and then both ran into a two-story building.

We pulled up in front of the door. I jumped out and flattened myself against the wall. My driver, PFC Randy Millhouse, came around the jeep. Just as he got in front of me, there came a loud rifle blast and the sickening sound of smashing flesh.

Randy was hit; his body jerked, face contorted, eyes wide looking at me as if saying, "What happened?" He fell into my arms and I laid him beside the wall. He was already unconscious or maybe dead. Blood oozed from above his flack jacket. The shot came from the window above us.

My rage boiled over at seeing young Randy shot. I felt crazy, as if in another body. Those dirty bastards. I checked inside the door. It opened into a stairway.

With my M-16 on full auto, I charged up the stairs knowing they could hear me coming but I didn't care. Just before I hit the top, two small caliber rounds smashed into the wall beside me. I looked up, but no one was there. I kept charging upward.

Reaching the top flight, I swung my rifle without looking around the corner and fired a burst. There was a high-pitched moan. When I stepped into the hallway, the other VC was going through a door at the end of the hall, slamming it behind him. I fired a long, full burst right through the door and wall, showering wood splinters and plaster everywhere. Again there was a yell. The building seemed to be empty apartments with several doors along the hall. It smelled old.

I raced down and kicked open what was left of the door. There was his bloody body, one eye staring back at me. I coughed from the plaster dust and gun smoke and then choked at the bloody carnage—half his head was gone.

At first I thought he was a boy, but then I saw he was just small like most Vietnamese. A torrent of emotions coursed through me—guilt for the killing, anger for Randy, sadness, and hate. Then an odd satisfaction of having to take a life, a "better he than me" philosophy.

I walked back to the first cong. A .38 revolver lay nearby, an issue for the Vietnamese police. There was something curious about the dead body. Long, black hair had fallen from beneath a head bandana. I rolled the body over with my foot. A shock wave went through me. It was the young girl on the bicycle that had thrown a grenade in my jeep a few days before.

She looked so peaceful, so young. I remembered her smile and wanted to tell her I was sorry. But at the same time, I wanted to shoot her body to pieces.

As fast as the feelings had come, they were gone. They were just two dead bodies of the enemy trying to kill me.

Back at the jeep, Randy was still alive. I called for help, and in short order, the medics and other patrols arrived. I never saw Randy Millhouse again, but I heard he survived and went home. Home...it seemed so long ago, a distant, gentle memory. I wondered if I'd ever see it again or return as Randy had with wounds of the body and soul, or in the ugly green body bag that had become infamous, invisible to the folks back home.

GOT MILK?

The large room was abuzz with over a hundred army, Marines, and airmen...all leaving Vietnam, including me. Cots in even rows held duffle bags and personal items the troops were taking home. You couldn't get more than six soldiers in one place and not have a poker game going on. Two beds had been pushed together and a game was in progress. I made a mental note to check it out later.

I threw my bag on an empty cot and looked for a familiar face. There was none, same as when I arrived fifteen months ago. Only now, the solemn, uneasy faces of arriving young men were replaced with handshakes, hugs, laughter, and tears. They all had won the lottery.

We would spend only one night in the building at the Bien Hoa airbase, and then others would take our place. U.S. troops were arriving and leaving daily. I sat down and looked over the two-day departure itinerary I'd received at the door. But the conversations going on around me were hard to ignore.

One was talking about his pregnant wife. "I'll be home for the birth of my baby," he said. Another talked about family and the holidays he missed. "I have two sisters and three brothers, and we'll all get together for a barbecue and swimming party." No one paid attention to his scarred face or his missing fingers.

Others were showing pictures and talking of girlfriends. One said, "He was my best friend, and I'm going to kick his ass for taking my girl while I was gone."

Me, I just wanted some real milk. I'd been raised on a dairy farm, and fresh, cold milk was a highlight of my youth and continued through my life. Watered-down powered milk was all the army gave us. Also, a good shower and Granny's cooking was another priority. Cold C-rations, going days without showers, and sleeping in water-lined foxholes would be bad memories.

The day was spent in line after line for paperwork, checking in our duffle bags and other personal items. Officers with special paperwork were hand-carrying Viet Cong rifles made in Russian or China. NVA pith helmets, red and yellow VC flags, VC officer's swords, bugles, and other war souvenirs had been sent ahead in trunks days before. Besides my own worn-out fatigues and MP helmet liner, all I had collected was a small, French-made .32 automatic pistol I had taken off a VC I had sent to Buddha heaven, or wherever it is they go.

Lunch and dinner weren't much different from any fire-based camp meal, though for some reason tasted much better; probably because it would be our last of its kind. And they were still serving that ugly brew of powered milk and water. After a few hours everything was arranged, and I received my final rotating orders. Departure for the world (USA) was the next morning at eight a.m.

That night, sleep didn't come easy. It wasn't the sleeping noises of all the men, but what was going on outside that made me nervous. American 105 shells were walking their way to a VC target some distance away. Once in a while sulfur smells from the artillery drifted into the building. The *whap, whap,* sounds of Huey gunships coming in and out, and a C-47, " Puff the magic dragon," took off.

Periodically, the pop of 60-milimeter VC mortars and the rattle of their 57-milimeter machine guns could be heard near the base. I waited for that one distinct sound of a 140-milimeter rocket bearing down on our building. There were stories of rocket attacks on the base and troops being killed just before boarding the plane. I pushed it out of my mind, focused on the thrill of being with my family again, and finally dozed off.

We were given the usual army wake up call at six a.m.; lights on, two sergeants yelling, "Up and at'um. Mess call at 0630. Your last delicious chow in Vietnam. You lucky bastards are going home today." Shouts of jubilation and sarcasm went up throughout the building: "Fin'ee, Vietnam…Mama, your baby boy is coming home."

Wouldn't you know our final meal was SOS, shit-on-a shingle, thick sausage gravy over toast, well-done scrambled eggs, and strong coffee. I just had toast and coffee and later would eat anything they served on the plane.

We stood in a long line waiting to board a Boeing 707, which stood a hundred yards away on the tarmac with a roll-up stair platform. At seven thirty in the morning, the heat and humidity was thick; my shirt already sticking to me. I thought about the last time I'd been on the tarmac. Jerry Pedersen and I came off the plane together from Travis Airbase and were shocked at the sweltering heat that greeted us. I remember he said something about returning home on this same field. He did…in a body bag.

There wasn't much conversation in line. It was almost eerie. Perhaps others were thinking about their buddies that were not returning with them. Dreadful memories were threatening to spoil the jubilation of the moment. I callously forgot them and returned to the excitement of leaving this place, of being in the presence of an American female stewardess with shapely legs in tight skirts, having a hot meal, and those tiny bottles of booze. The line began to move, and the thrill started to churn within me. But what I really craved was a glass of cold, real milk.

At the door of the plane, we were greeted by a pretty, smiling stewardess wearing a baby-blue skirt suit and pillbox hat. I grabbed an aisle seat, hoping to be served first and have a view of the activities. The cabin smelled fresh, soft music floated from overhead. For the first time since arriving in Vietnam in 1966, I was beginning to feel like a human being in a civilized world.

Nervous chatter and excited flirtations began almost immediately toward the stewardesses: "Where have you been all my life?" "Didn't we date in high school?" "We gotta quit meeting like this." The women smiled politely, probably having heard every line in the book.

After the initial ecstasy of being in the presence of women and the familiarity of the cabin, the troops settled into their polite, military manner of "Yes, ma'am" and "No, miss." As we taxied to the runway, the men were quiet as the ladies went through their seat belt and exits routine. But the real elation came when the aircraft actually lifted off the ground: loud applause, whistles, shouting, cheers of exuberance, and celebration rolled throughout the cabin. Some men even broke down and cried. I could see the blonde stewardess in her jump-seat at the bulkhead wiping tears from her eyes. It may have been her first flight to Vietnam or she just never got used to the pure joy and sadness of men leaving the heartbreak of the war. It even got to me.

As the plane banked, I could see the beautiful, green countryside below. Under that emerald canopy filled with exotic birds, plants, peaceful rivers, and farmland were men trying to kill each other in the worse possible ways. Somewhere down there was my squad, carrying on the war without me. Guilt made its way into my party, and I felt remorse for leaving them behind. They were young and had been dependent on my experience and guidance. Like the time we left a village and the Cong ambushed us from behind. Amid the surprise attack, panic struck until I got them on line to form defense fighting positions.

The terror came rushing back. I felt smothered, flush, and hot, and it was hard to breathe. I turned on the overhead air and directed it onto my face. The stewardess came by, and seeing my discomfort asked if she could do anything. I said no, realizing I was having an anxiety attack, stressed from mixed emotions. When someone is killed or wounded, an odd feeling of callousness occurs. *It's better he than me.* I was glad to be in the plane, returning to a world where life made sense.

After reaching cruising altitude, the stewardess began serving drinks and taking food orders. The blonde I'd seen sitting in the jump-seat earlier leaned down with her notepad and ask what I wanted. Her nametag said Mandy. Her perfume was intoxicating, and I wanted to pull her down into my arms.

"Do you have real milk? You know, not the powered mix?" I asked.

"Yes, we do, in the cartons. May I get you one?"

"Is it cold?"

She nodded yes.

"Then may I have about three cartons?"

"I'll see what I can do." She smiled, took my order, and left.

Later, with eyes closed, I savored the cold, thick milk, letting it flow slowly over my tongue and down my throat, taking my time with each swallow straight from the carton. It was the best taste I'd had in fifteen months. Being raised on a dairy farm I knew the pleasure of drinking pure, cold milk coming off the stainless-steel cooling system. At my grandmother's home, there were large family gatherings with wonderful home cooking and plenty of cold milk. There is no greater environment of contentment and security than having a family together, the world in perfect order.

Food and alcohol had put the men in a state of fatigue, mentally and physically. Most dozed off. The cabin grew quiet, except for an occasional snore. Somewhere behind me, I heard muttering and then clear words from a bad dream, "They're coming! They're coming!" After that the long flight was mostly in silence, and I too drifted off into a restless sleep.

We landed in Oakland, the home base for World Airways and the military processing center for returning servicemen. There was no welcome home gathering, no flags, no banners or posters declaring the country's devotion to our troops. It was just a long, quiet walk to a large building some distance from the plane. Inside the facilities were barracks, commissary, barber shop, tailor store for new uniforms, and the processing room.

We'd have to spend another couple of hours there, doing more paperwork for getting back into the U.S., and flight vouchers for our final leg home. Some men got haircuts; some got new uniforms fitted for required travel. I received my honorable discharge from service, having completed my tour of duty in Vietnam. I also received my new dress greens uniform along with the campaign medals I'd been awarded. When I left there, I held my head a little higher and walked a little taller.

From there, we were on our own. The servicemen would make their way to San Francisco International for flights home all across the U.S. Depending on flight times, some would be spending the night. Others, like me, shared a cab to SFO to catch flights that evening.

I hadn't called my parents, wanting to surprise them. I would just show up on the doorstep, an exhilarating moment for all of us.

At the airport, we said our good-byes, good lucks, and went our separate ways. I found the commuter airline counter to Modesto and checked in. I had three hours to kill, so I headed for the bar.

The bartender set a napkin in front of me and asked what I wanted. Daniels and beer back; something that would really take the edge off. When he placed the drinks down, he said, "Just returned from 'Nam?"

"Yeah, how'd you know?"

"'Nam campaign ribbons." He looked down. "And your hands are still shaking. This one is on me, Soldier. Welcome home."

It was the first and only drink that would be bought for me after returning home. For the next three hours, I listened to the music and made small talk with the bartender, feeling better and better, then a little fuzzy. I looked at the clock and realized I'd been sitting there three hours. I rushed to the commuter airline counter and asked about my flight.

"I'm sorry, it just left. We have been calling it for 20 minutes," one of the two girls said.

"I have to be on that plane. I just got back from Vietnam and I'm going home!" Tears began to swell up. "Can you call it back?"

The brunette said she'd try and went to the phone. Returning, she apologized and both girls also had tears, one saying, "The aircraft was too far onto the tarmac to come back."

"When's the next flight," I asked.

"Not until tomorrow morning."

I was numb. What to do now? My cousin lived in San Carlos. I didn't have his phone number, so I took the twenty-minute cab ride to his house, praying he'd be home. He was shocked to see me. After telling him my airport story, he volunteered to drive to Modesto.

We arrived at my mother's home at one a.m. and woke them up. When Mom came to the door and saw me, she screamed, cried, and hugged me. The racket brought in my sister and stepfather, and they joined the unexpected homecoming. It was one of the happiest moments in my life.

HOMECOMING

When I opened my eyes, I jerked straight up in bed. It was a strange room, with flowered curtains over the window, wallpaper, and a sitting chair in the corner. In seconds the event of my homecoming came rolling back. It was my mother's guestroom. She and her new husband had moved there while I was in 'Nam. Back there, I'd wake up to the smell of canvas, sandbags, and gun oil in my hooch. I'd grab some bennies, wash them down with a shot of whisky, get my rifle, and go find the lieutenant. I was a civilian now, no one to give me orders, send me on patrol, no wearing muddy clothes or cleaning my rifle. Now, there was the aroma of fresh coffee and bacon. I got dressed and headed to the kitchen.

Mom was at the stove and turned when I entered. "Coffee?" she said. Without waiting for an answer, she poured a cup and placed it in front of me, remembering I liked it black. The hot, mellow flavor tasted much better than army coffee. She had made the perfect Okie breakfast: eggs fried in bacon grease, biscuits and gravy, and fried potatoes. I'd never tasted anything so good.

"How did you sleep?" she asked.

"Not bad," I lied, for I'd tossed and turned half the night. Only after I'd drunk a half pint of whisky from my overnight bag did I finally fall asleep.

"It's going to be hot today. You might want to go to the lake and relax a bit."

What a great idea. I could get together with friends or relatives take some beer and maybe meet girls like the old days. How odd. Here I was drinking coffee with Mom, when three days before, I had been in Vietnam wondering if I'd live to see the next day or if I'd end up lying face down in a mud hole. I waited for a rocket to hit, waking me up and blowing this wonderful dream all to hell. It was a warm feeling talking with Mom about family and friends, catching up on the latest. But overall, not much had really changed; folks still lived and worked at the same places. I'd been gone for fifteen months, but it seemed like years.

After breakfast, I returned to my room and dug through the box of clothes. My old things, some white T-shirts and Levis, assorted shirts, my favorite pegged pants, and high school letter jacket and red and white football jersey, number seventy-four. My dream of playing college football had never happened. Why not now? I took the thought to the window and looked out. Though it was morning, heat waves were already coming off the street, leaves on the trees were still, and two women were walking by. I could enroll at the JC for the fall semester and sign up for football. My life was starting new; everything was here for me.

I'd sent most of my pay home, so my bank account was decent; and along with my discharge money, it was enough to buy a car. It felt good being in a position to make choices, something I hadn't had since graduating from high school. I decided against going to the lake, but rather wait for the weekend to see about getting the family together like we used to do.

That evening, I went to a place called the Office, a bar in my mom's neighborhood where patrons joked about telling the wife or friends they were going to the Office. It was nice being in a place not filled with uniformed soldiers. Couples were dancing to music from a jukebox while others visited and laughed in booths and tables. I took an open stool at the bar and ordered a drink and then watched the dancers.

When the weekend arrived, my family and I gathered and took food and beer for a picnic at the lake. The crowds of people, power boats, and the rustle of the leaves in nearby trees made me a little jumpy, but I loved every moment of being there. My two cousins Novell, Everett, and I talked of doing some hunting and fishing. Tomorrow we would go into the mountains and hunt gray squirrels with shot guns and .22s, and next weekend, go fishing. I was enthused at the thought; something I had always enjoyed. It had been a great day, though everyone got sunburned. My upper body was already bronze from the hot, tropical sun of Southeast Asia, but my legs were ghostly white.

Early Sunday morning, the three of us drove into the Sierra Mountain range nearby. Novell pulled his pickup truck off the dirt road into a clearing and killed the engine. Everett and I took the shotguns, .22s, and boxes of shells from the truck bed. When Novell joined us, we split up the ammo.

"Just beyond that little ridge is some thick brush and trees; it's usually crawling with grays. You should be good at this," said Novell as he looked at me, smiling.

"I need a machine gun." They both laughed. I had brought my .22 semi-automatic rifle with a ten-round clip. We lined up and checked each other's positions with me on the right end. As we started to walk, I became uneasy from the moment I'd taken the .22 in my hands and jacked in the first round.

Before, the beginning of the hunt had always been the height of exhilaration, but something was different now. I found myself looking up into the trees, down at the ground, then all around, and repeating the surveillance maneuver over and over again.

I was looking for anything out of the ordinary, like movement in the trees when there was no wind, a trip-wire to a VC booby trap; a brown, broken branch when all the foliage was green could conceal a booby trap.

A sudden noise in the brush to my right shot fear and adrenaline from my head to my feet. I flipped off the safety, squatted and came around with the rifle in one smooth action ready to shoot. A huge, gray squirrel scurried across the ground and disappeared behind a tree. I froze ... *Charlie's here; I can feel him.* The leaves began to swish from a breeze. I swung around and aimed up, patrolling my rifle from tree to tree.

"Hey!" yelled Everett. "What are you doing over there?"

I turned the rifle on him and was a split second away from pulling the trigger, when he hollered, "No, no!" Both men hit the ground, yelling my name for me not to shoot. *I moved the rifle from one man to the other, to let those gook-face VC know I had them ... one move and these bastards were dead men.* "No, stop, stop." *Why was the lieutenant calling out my name instead of Sergeant ... the idiot.* The voices kept repeating over and over in my head. What was happening?

Slowly the images of my two cousins came into focus, their distorted faces became clear. It was Novell and Everett on the ground, *not the VC.* I lowered the rifle and stared at them. As quickly as the flashback had come, it was gone, leaving my heart racing, hands shaking. I walked over to them and Everett began scooting backward, eyes wide.

"God, I'm so sorry, I don't know what happened to me. I was back there ... I thought ... "

"You're okay now, right?" Novell said, getting to his feet.

"Yeah, yeah, I'm fine, but I can't believe what just happened. There have been nightmares before, but nothing like this." I had ruined the hunting trip. We loaded everything back into the truck and drove to a bar in a small town nearby, where we proceeded to get loaded and laughed about the scary incident. I could have shot them, but it really wasn't funny and I never went hunting again.

The following Saturday morning, the three of us drove out into the country to one of the many rivers near Everett's home in the town of Patterson. All week I'd been looking forward to the outing. This was something more relaxing and peaceful; it brought back splendid memories of fishing with my family and buddies.

We had a large cooler full of beer, a quart of Early Times bourbon, chips, and sandwiches. We found a sandy beach on the river bank and set up our supplies. Novell and Everett grabbed their fishing gear, some beers, and went several yards down river. The sandy bank tapered down to the weeds at the water's edge, a perfect fishing spot. I prepared and baited my line with a live grub worm like I had done hundreds of times, tossed it out a reasonable distance, and sat down in a low folding chair. I leaned back and let the rising sun warm my face, and I sipped bourbon from a paper cup, easing it down with a cold beer … life was good.

After sometime without any fishing activity, I dozed off to the harmonious sounds of flowing water. *A tug on my line woke me up. A low fog had rolled in; visibility was only a few feet. I sat up when the line tugged again. Pulling it taut, I began reeling it in. Just below the water's surface was something strange, white, and round. I leaned down for a closer look. Suddenly it popped up ... a decaying head of a VC soldier, a black hole in the forehead. I screamed and fell backward. The water turned red as more bodies drifted to the river bank. I tried to move backward, but my feet slipped in the sand. Then came the deafening sound of automatic weapons, grenades popping, and screams of dying men. The VC sat up out of the water, small pieces of white flesh peeled from the scull face, "You good shot, GI," he said. I put my hands over my ears, lowered my head between knees, and wailed in panic, trying to block out the horrifying noise. I heard my voice, "No, no! Go away."*

Hands grabbed my shoulders, and then my hands were pulled away from my ears.

"Stop it, you crazy bastard, its okay," said Everett.

I opened my eyes to find comfort from the friendly hands and familiar voice. I was still in the chair, the sun bright and warm, dark green water moved gently by. It had happened again, another day mare. My stomach felt tight, mouth dry.

I found the can of beer and Early Times beside my chair and downed them both. That was the last time I went fishing too.

COLLEGE FOOTBALL

When school started in September, I enrolled in Modesto Junior College. I fit right in with students of all ages. I'd played four years of high school football and dreamed of playing for a major college. But instead, I got married at nineteen and had a baby girl at twenty. After returning home I received divorce papers which I gladly signed. Maybe playing JC football would be a new start. My physical condition was the best ever, considering what my body had been through. Since being home, I ate everything within reach. The weeks before school started, I weight trained and ran wind sprints at the Modesto High School football field. By the time practice began, I had put on fifteen rock-hard pounds.

Preseason training went well and I made first team defensive linebacker. I was older and more mature than the other players and learned the play-book quickly. The daily practices were exhausting for most of the players, but after hiking miles in the jungle heat with sixty pounds of gear, it was just playtime for me. I dated the cheerleaders and went to parties, but I never stayed late or drank too much.

Our first opponent from upstate was a home night game. That evening while suiting up in the gym, I went back in time to Vietnam and our tent and sandbag hooch, getting ready for my first patrol. We checked our weapons, ammo, and gear for the mission. Back then I was reminded of suiting up for football games. Now it was the other way around, a good and thankful feeling. I couldn't help smiling.

Back in the fifties, my high school football team had played on the same college field since we did not have our own stadium. The night was exhilarating, like starting life where I'd left off, the smell of dew-covered turf, the lights, the glamour of specta-tors, and band music. The smell of popcorn and hot dogs drifted onto the field like I remembered in high school.

Just before kickoff, the familiar butterflies came and went once the ball was in the air. I moved down-field at a sprinter's pace, a hunter's instinct...find the ball.

The game was more physical and violent than I remembered in high school, elbows to the ribs, fore-arms to the head, hit the man anywhere to get an advantage. Yet throwing a man to the ground without doing more harm to him was kids' play to me.

I dealt out vicious and punishing tackles, a game of hand-to-hand combat without weapons, close-quarter aggression. The air was heavy with pungent body odor and harsh equipment; the taste of blood and sweat was in the corner of my mouth.

Through a forest of arms and legs, I zeroed in on the ball tucked neatly into a ribcage. I struggled, fighting my way through an army of bodies.

Suddenly, without warning, just as it had happened many times before, I was transferred back to another time and place, a small clearing in a Vietnam jungle.

I pulled a slight, brown-faced Viet Cong to me to put him out of the fight quickly. He's on the ground, face twisted in horrid pain, eyes squeezed tight in agony and finally death.

I move quickly to the next dark figure, propelled by a fusion of fear and hatred, my hatchet and .45 pistol ready for the next victim. I dodge his bayonet charge. We collide, roll to the ground, each franticly maneuvering for the kill. I let out a war cry, a scream of terror, a rally of courage. One hand on his throat, the other free with the hatchet, my pistol lost. I pushed him deeper into the mud, then one swift motion with the weapon. He lies limp with just a wince as his final breath.

I looked into the darkness but see only flickering images, mostly shadows. Where are my men? Then a high-pitched sound becoming louder and louder; it's a whistle. More VC charging! Hands tug and pull at my shoulder. I scream, turn, and lash out.

A voice called, "Play's over. Get off. Play's over." I didn't know where I was. Slowly a face comes into focus. What was a man in a zebra-striped shirt doing in Vietnam? Why was I laying on top of a kid in a football uniform?

Gradually, I melt back...it's a football game. The sound is a referee's whistle blowing the play dead, and the hands on me are my teammates pulling me off.

Slowly I got to my feet, stunned, dazed. Mud and sweat dripped from my face and hands. I look at the figure curled on the ground. My God, I tried to kill that poor kid.

I remembered. I had hit the ball carrier so hard his helmet flew off, and I saw the slanted eyes and olive skin of an Asian man. I had him clean off his feet and tried to drive him into the ground.

My teammates stared at me like someone they didn't recognize, a madman, certainly not one of their own.

"You okay, son?" The ref asked the boy now up on one elbow, head hanging, a low moan seeping from his lips.

"I think so," he finally said, his words stuttering like a drunk. Slowly he got to his feet, eyes blank.

"Take him out, Coach." The ref shouted toward the other bench. Two of his teammates helped him off the field. Coach Pat pulled me from the game too.

"You okay? You hit him pretty hard. Did you hurt yourself?" Coach said, bending in front of me. "Are you sure you're all right? What was all the yelling about? That's not necessary you know. Sounds like you were trying to kill someone."

"Yeah, I'm fine. Just sit me out a couple of plays. I'll be ready."

I tried to understand what had happened to me. The close engagement of violence and the Asian face had triggered a flashback. My nerves were still detonating inside; my hands shook and my legs were weak.

These episodes had come before. I had wrestled with the grisly memories, trying to entomb them somewhere in a cavern of my mind, but the apparitions were determined to stay.

Back in the game, my enthusiasm lost, I just went through the motions until the final gun sounded. The following Monday, I quit the team. It was too much too soon. My hopes and dreams as a young man still lay somewhere on the soft ground of a steaming jungle. I could only hope and pray that someday they would rise up from the smolders of hell and embrace me once again.

THE DRIFTER

After I quit the football team, I lost interest in my classes and dropped out of school. It seemed things were not working out for me in Modesto. Obviously I couldn't play football or do the things I used to. I felt like a machine running at high speed, ready to explode at any moment.

Restless, I drove to LA and hooked up with Kelly, an old girlfriend. She was young and pretty; we were soon married. Every weekend we went out drinking with friends. I had a truck driving job, but got a DUI coming home from a bar one night, resulting in having my driver's license suspended.

We decided to move to Las Vegas where I could get a new driver's license. The first day we found an apartment, and in a short time got jobs in different casinos. I became a security guard and she a waitress.

Things were going good, or at least I thought they were. I was playing poker whenever I wasn't working and Kelly spent time with her new friends. But the time apart eroded our marriage. Because of my drinking, nerves, and nightmares, we grew apart and she left me, later we divorced. I sank into a whirlpool of despair and feelings of unworthiness. I drank myself to sleep and began missing work, barely keeping my job. But it was the job that would give me my five minutes of fame. The only good memory I would take out of Las Vegas.

As a security officer, I patrolled the parking lots and the hotel rooms behind the casino. My vehicle looked like a police car, very impressive. The only difference was the drunk behind the wheel. Many nights I came to work with a hangover.

One night, it was raining buckets. I parked where I could see the whole parking lot and listened to the rain pound the car like a billion bugs on a Texas highway. The heater didn't work and the inside air was cold enough to see my breath. I pulled my collar up around my neck and slumped deeper into the seat trying to sleep. Things couldn't be worse, or at least I thought they couldn't.

A call came over the radio. "Proceed to the casino entrance and secure a limo parked there and stay with it until the VIPs return." I stood near the limo as curious onlookers passed by. The rain was cold and walking around to stay warm didn't help.

After a couple of hours, my annoyance spilled over. My jacket was soaked through, I was freezing, and the VIPs were wearing on my patience. *How dare they make me stand out here like a servant?* On top of everything else, I would have killed for a drink. I thought about Kelly and how our lives had unraveled so quickly. I wondered where she was, if she was okay. Did she want a divorce?

My hand radio cracked on, snapping me back. "The VIPs are coming out now."

A group of six hefty guys pushed through the doors, all dressed in black. In the middle was a taller man, also wearing black.

When the group drew closer, I was stunned to see it was Elvis Presley. He was gorgeous. That might sound odd coming from another guy, but that's the only word to use. His hair was so black it looked blue, his face and hands were tan, his eyes and teeth, bright and white. He was tall and tapered, bigger than life. When he looked at me, I could only muster a nod.

He nodded back and said, "How'ya doing?"

"Fine, thank you." I said with a goofy smile.

He smiled back and told one of his aids to take care of me. One of the men came over, pulling something from inside of his expensive jacket. It was a hundred-dollar bill. That was it, my five minutes of fame. He drove off into the night rain and I never saw him again except on TV or the movies. I had been elevated that night just being in his presence. I was struck by the way he carried himself, with pride and dignity, yet with all his success he was humble enough to speak to a security guard. I suddenly became inspired to make more of myself than a drunken gambler, whining over a woman who didn't want me. I wanted to be a better person and declared that I could at least start by being a sober gambler.

Shortly after meeting Elvis, I quit my job and began playing poker. But to do this, I had to straighten myself out. The next day I headed for the poker tables sober, to build a bankroll. I played day and night, drinking only coffee and juices instead of booze, eating and sleeping sparingly. I filled two shoeboxes full of cash and called it quits. It was time to go. I decided to give this place up and head back to L.A. where I at least had family and friends.

I returned to LA and played poker in the Gardena card clubs and private games. But being back with old friends, old habits followed. With the drinking came the loneliness and restlessness. I longed for some kind of stability. Since I hadn't seen my dad after returning from Nam, I went to Illinois where he lived with his new wife. We had never been close, him being the silent type. But he was a strong, kindly man. I had always compared him to Gary Cooper in looks and manner. In his youth, he'd been a working cowboy and rodeo rider in Oklahoma and he loved talking about it. We often sat around drinking and talking about old times of when we lived on the dairy ranch. We became friends and I loved him dearly. Dad worked at a steel factory and got me a job there moving rolls of steel sheeting with a forklift. I bought another car, but I crashed it when hitting some black ice, and I flew off the road while driving home drunk one night. I was banged up some, but the car was totaled. Thank God no one else was involved. After the wreck, I felt my stay had been long enough, that my life was much the same no matter where I went.

Whatever it was I was searching for wasn't here either. It was time to return to LA. My sister invited me to stay with her. One morning after an all-night drinking bout, I got a blind impulse to leave it all behind and bought a one-way ticket to Hawaii and was off on another adventure.

Hawaii was exciting and beautiful. For a short time, I lived in a hippy commune on the beach, but I soon tired of that and returned to Waikiki and took a job at a beachfront hotel. The nightclub life and the hotel beaches were a year-long marathon of booze, women, and poker.

"You would love my little family, I have five dogs," the conversations would go.

"They even sleep in my bed." *I like animals, but not that much.*

"Maybe I could call my boss and try to extend my vacation and stay in your place." *I like you sweetheart, but your time is up.*

"I'm here with my mom and dad and they would die if they knew what I was doing with you."

"How old are you?"

"Seventeen." *Ahh...*

I met a couple of woman poker players, pretty and sharp players, but they were too much like me;

unsettled lives going nowhere. I played poker in hotel suites, beautiful homes in the mountains, seedy bar back rooms, or an old hotel downtown Hono.

I was getting so tired of this kind of life, but I was always searching for the woman that would fulfill my dreams for a wife.

A friend of mine took a government job in the Marshall Islands, which sounded very exiting to me. With my military police security clearance, it was easy to obtain a position as a U.S. Marshall, securing missile tracking stations on the atolls. But there were no single women, only married couples with families. This made me want a family even more. There was no social life for the bachelor employee. Besides work, all we did was play poker and drink. I lasted six months and returned to Hawaii, then back to LA. My life was an avalanche hurling downhill, out of control. But for this lost soul of a man without purpose or direction, things were about to change.

DREAMS DO COME TRUE

In 1973, after having dinner in a family restaurant one evening, I went into the adjoining cocktail lounge for a drink. There was a pretty woman
holding a fluffy puppy talking to a guy seated at
the bar. Though my interest was in the girl, the
pup was the perfect introduction. I asked if I could
hold the puppy, and we started talking. It was the
strangest conversation I'd ever had in my life. She
said her birthday was in October. I said, "Me too."
She asked what day. I said, "The twelfth." She
said, "Me too." I had been divorced five years. She
said, "Me too." She had been married twice. I said,
"Me too." She worked out at Jack LaLanne Gym.
"Me too, I'm a trainer there."

The conversation continued that way the rest of the evening. It was so natural, so comfortable. She was about five feet tall with long, dark hair, nice curves, a beautiful smile, and a wonderful sense of humor. We chatted for some time before I realized we hadn't introduced ourselves. She said her name was Sylvia, and I smartly said, "Me too." It was too good to pass up.

The following evening, she invited me to her home for a steak dinner and to meet her three girls. *Three girls!* I wasn't ready for kids. However, we had just met and were only friends. What harm in meeting her family?

The next night was the beginning of becoming a new man. The girls were older than I had anticipated: Lena, age nine, Lindy, twelve, and Cindy, fifteen, all well mannered, fun, humorous, and beautiful like their mother. I loved them all immediately, and they accepted me just as quickly. Nothing had ever felt so right and familiar since my youth, the harmony of a family that I wanted to be a part of. Eight months later, we were married on our birthdays in our church in Arcadia, California. I moved into her house, bringing with me everything I owned in my old Pontiac. Now I had a wife, three daughters, and my first real home. We had our anniversary and birthdays on the same day. What more could a man ask for?

Unknowingly, the four of them helped with my post-traumatic syndrome disorder with a sense of humor and unfussy manner. I stopped drinking, though my nerves were still frayed. Once while try-ing to retrieve a newspaper from the rack, I pulled the handle before the money fell through and it didn't open. My rage flared up and I kicked and cussed that stupid rack. All four of the girls were in the car laughing. I was embarrassed. Public phones also became the target of my madness when they took my dime. My new wife had a challenge on her hands, teaching me to be patient.

Sylvia was a bail bondsman and used a pager, which she put in a charger at night that cast off a small glow. A wig had been placed on a Styrofoam head sitting next to the charger. One time when I woke up in the middle of the night and saw that, I hollered, "The VC is here!" When the nightmares came, she was there to hold and comfort me.

Sylvia recognized my interest in reading and writing and encouraged me to enter college under the GI education bill. We both enrolled in Citrus College and had a couple of classes together. We were the oldest students in most of our classes. To my surprise, I loved school, even the homework. Journalism and creative writing became my passion.

We shared a sense of adventure, like buying prop-erty in northern Nevada, sight unseen, moving there four years later without having jobs. Cindy, who at this time was nineteen and in college, was sad about us leaving, but choose to stay in L.A.

In Nevada, a motel became our home until escrow closed on our new house. Within a week I got a job with a construction company. I became part of the community building two schools and two banks, a library and a casino at Lake Tahoe. Meanwhile, Sylvia and her new best friend, Marlene, whose children were the same age as ours, ran around town having lunches, starting bible study groups and embarrassing our kids,. One day while riding past the school, Sylvia stood up waving from the sun roof while Marlene blew the horn.

Gardnerville was a very exciting place to live. Wild mustangs and deer roamed the hills near our home. Unusual events took place around the Carson Valley all the time, like camels racing, a whistle-off contest, cow pasture boxing, a round-up with a branding, and barbecue at a casino owner's ranch. There was an authentic wagon train that started back east somewhere that ended up in the Nevada Carson Valley Days parade. All these events we did as a family. We became involved with a square-dancing group and joined a church. We met some wonderful people that became lifelong friends.

Lindy and Lena loved riding their horses on an open range and went trick-or-treating on horseback with a group from 4-H. They also spent time in the mountains, rock climbing and hanging out at the lakes.

When the girls settled into school, Sylvia and I took writing classes at the junior college. They say to write about what you know, and the one thing I really knew was poker. By then, poker had become popular in the casinos, and I began playing in tournaments and writing articles about them for the local newspaper. I self-published a how-to poker book that sold in the casinos and local stores. Sylvia started working as a waitress in a casino at Lake Tahoe, and I played poker waiting for her to get off work. Before long, the free sodas became free booze, and I was on my way again.

From the beginning, Sylvia had said she wouldn't tolerate me going to the bars without her. The first time I did, this little pussy cat became a wild tiger. She came into the bar and gave me a right-cross to the kisser, saying "Get home and get your things. We're through." Ashamed and distraught over my weakness, I went home immediately to make things right. But she wasn't so forgiving with my drinking problem. It was her way or the highway. Finally grasping the fact that I was an alcoholic and needed help, I went to Alcoholics Anonymous, and we became more involved in church and Bible studies. Turbulent waters became smooth.

After being in northern Nevada for twenty years, we move to Palm Desert, California. But six of those years were spent traveling and working across the United States, seeing all fifty states, some islands, Mexico, and Canada, traveling in a fifth-wheel, a custom van, by sea and air.

In Palm Desert, we live in a country club where we golf, swim and are active in several clubs. I also reestablished my passion for writing by joining a writing group. With their guidance and discipline, I published short stories and rewrote my poker book that sold to a publisher. Since I am of Native American heritage, I became active with my Chickasaw Nation, going to meetings and serving on the local council.

Without question, my optimistic wife saved me from a life of alcohol, aimless drifting, and possible doom. For you veterans that are still struggling with PTSD, I want you to know there is so much in life to enjoy. You must strive to seek peace at all cost. It's not easy as you can see by my story. The ghosts will never completely leave, so don't even try to think they will. Tell your stories and be proud you served and survived. I'd like to suggest that believing in a higher power will help, and a good woman wouldn't hurt either. Peace and comfort is not inside a bottle or drugs.

I dare not think where my life was headed had I not walked into the lounge that night. It was her encouragement and support that compelled me to write these Vietnam stories that lay lurking in my dark side for over forty-four years.

1978 Gardnerville, Nevada - From left to right: Lindy,
Cindy, Sylvia sitting on the rail and Lena.

ABOUT THE AUTHOR

Ted Pannell was conceived in Oklahoma, popped out in Tulare, California, and raised in Modesto. He is Chickasaw Indian on his mother's side, English on his father's.

Raised on a dairy farm, he learned about life and death caring for farm animals. Camping and hunting with relatives, he was taught about guns and outdoor survival skills.

In 1965 he volunteered for the draft and served fifteen months in Vietnam with the 18th MP Group. After his tour, he traveled and played poker. He went to college on his GI bill majoring in Journalism and Literature and is a member of The Author's Guild, Palm Springs Writer's Guild and a writer's group.